RFID Field Guide

RFID Field Guide

Deploying Radio Frequency Identification Systems

Manish Bhuptani • **Shahram Moradpour**

Sun Microsystems Press
A Prentice Hall Title

**PRENTICE
HALL**
PTR   Prentice Hall Professional Technical Reference
Upper Saddle River, NJ • Boston• Indianapolis • San Francisco
New York • Toronto • Montreal • London • Munich • Paris • Madrid
Capetown • Sydney • Tokyo • Singapore • Mexico City

The publisher offers excellent discounts on this book when ordered in quantity for bulk purchases or special sales, which may include electronic versions and/or custom covers and content particular to your business, training goals, marketing focus, and branding interests. For more information, please contact:

U.S. Corporate and Government Sales
(800) 382-3419
corpsales@pearsontechgroup.com

For sales outside the U.S., please contact:

International Sales
international@pearsoned.com

This Book Is Safari Enabled.

The Safari® Enabled icon on the cover of your favorite technology book means the book is available through Safari Bookshelf. When you buy this book, you get free access to the online edition for 45 days.

Safari Bookshelf is an electronic reference library that lets you easily search thousands of technical books, find code samples, download chapters, and access technical information whenever and wherever you need it.

To gain 45-day Safari Enabled access to this book:

- Go to http://www.phptr.com/safarienabled
- Complete the brief registration form
- Enter the coupon code HWJF-100K-7N5A-J6KK-WN2R

If you have difficulty registering on Safari Bookshelf or accessing the online edition, please e-mail customer-service@safaribooksonline.com.

Visit us on the Web: www.phptr.com

Library of Congress Catalog Number: 2004115642

ISBN 0-13-185355-4
Text printed in the United States on recycled paper at Phoenix Book Tech.
First printing, February 2005
Sun Microsystems Press Publisher: Myrna Rivera

Sun Microsystems Press
A Prentice Hall Title

To Paree for your infinite wisdom and support,
and to Ryan, Dylan, and Megan for the
most enjoyable and encouraging massages.
—Shahram

To my parents and my wife Priya for their support
and encouragement. To my kids Sonam and
Mihir—you make it all worthwhile.
—Manish

CONTENTS

ABOUT THE AUTHORS

Shahram Moradpour is CEO and co-founder of Cleritec Systems based in Silicon Valley. Cleritec provides RFID solutions for manufacturing, retail, and healthcare companies. Prior to Cleritec, Shahram was Senior Director of Market Development at Sun Microsystems where he oversaw Sun's alliances with more than 450 partners. He also sponsored and directed numerous emerging technology projects with Fortune 500 companies. He holds Master and Bachelor of Science degrees in Computer Science from UCLA.

Manish Bhuptani is President and co-founder of Cleritec Systems. Prior to Cleritec he was Director of Market Development at Sun Microsystems where he grew Sun's market presence in emerging and established markets. He has also worked as a management consultant at A.T. Kearney where he advised Fortune 500 companies on business strategy, and as a software engineer at IBM. He holds an MBA from the University of California, Berkeley, an MS in Computer Engineering from Purdue University, and a BE in Electrical Engineering from The Cooper Union.

PREFACE

As the number of devices attached to the Network[1] has grown exponentially, the value of the Network and the benefits of being attached to it have increased dramatically as well. First, thousands of mainframes and mini computers shared business data. Then, millions of PCs connected to the Network did the same, followed by tens of millions of mobile phones and handhelds, which spawned more high-value networked services such as email on any device, instant messaging, push-to-talk, file sharing, business-to-business commerce, and many more. Today, shared applications and services are the norm. But the revolution is just beginning. Soon, billions of devices—each with its own digital heartbeat—will connect to the Network. Many will utilize a single powerful technology: Radio Frequency Identification (RFID).

---

[1] The Network here refers to a collection of computing and communications devices connected to exchange data. A couple of decades ago, the Network only meant a collection of mainframes or mini computers connected through dedicated lines. In the early '90s, the Internet was added to the Network, and since then has been widely used as a synonym for the Network. Now the Network includes not only computers connected with one another, but also mobile phones, PDAs (Personal Digital Assistants), embedded computers in objects such as cars, and even objects with RFID tags. All these things are capable of some type of data exchange via the Network.

RFID tags will be found embedded in everything from cereal boxes to prescription medicines to parts of an aircraft to a variety of other machinery. These tags, when in proximity of the right type of sensors, will broadcast information about the objects they are embedded in—dimensions, whereabouts, identification numbers, history of temperatures they were exposed to, and many other static and dynamic characteristics. Many sensors located in hospitals, manufacturing plants, stores, or automobiles will collect this data, aggregate it, and route it to various humans and decision support systems.

The benefits derived from offering services based on such information will be tremendous. Businesses will run more efficiently and consumers will experience better and more innovative services. For example, instead of a grocery store losing sales because of consumers not finding meat in stock, the RFID tags in the meat packages being bought will tell the store's in-house sensors that the shelves are more than half empty, triggering a reorder to the supplier. The supplier, armed with the latest information about the location of his meat shipments (thanks to RFID-based pallets used in trucks connected to the central facility via a Global Positioning System), will direct the nearest available shipment to the store. As the truck carrying the goods is being unloaded at the loading dock, the RFID tags in those boxes will alert the store's inventory system, which in turn will alert the stocking clerk to get ready to stock the shelves. The time saved due to automatic detection of low stock levels and corresponding delivery means that the grocery store would not run out of meat, increasing profits.

In addition, the tags will have data about the temperatures the boxes were exposed to in transit. If the refrigeration system in the truck malfunctioned, exposing some of the packages to higher than recommended temperatures, the tags will help the store clerk identify and separate out packages containing spoilt goods. Detection of possibly spoilt goods means that the customers would not have to suffer the consequences, averting a potential health disaster and liability for the store.

These are the promises of RFID. But which of these promises will prove true, and which will be revealed as hype? How can a simple RFID tag make all this possible? What should you, the reader, be doing to embrace this phenomenon of an "RFID-enabled world"? How does this RFID technology work? What types of applications are possible and who is adopting the technology? What is the payoff for an organization from RFID adoption? What are the drivers and barriers to adoption?

What is the next step for an organization trying to figure out how to proceed with an RFID deployment? We are sure many such questions have come to your mind by now.

We hope to answer these questions in this book. Our experience in the industry has exposed us to the latest software being developed at the tiniest software start-ups and to the business and IT needs of the largest Fortune 500 companies. In the process, we have also had a bird's eye view of many new technologies and new applications of existing technologies. We have seen many technology innovations that were high on promise and low on substance. We have also met many vendors who flocked to capitalize on those innovations only to fail, as there were no sizable revenue or business models associated with them. At the same time, we have met many customers who routinely use cutting-edge technology as a competitive weapon to strengthen their business.

As we worked with companies that promised to apply RFID to solve complex business problems and customers who looked at this technology to help them leapfrog the competition, we realized that some of the fundamental questions customers were asking were not being addressed sufficiently, placing customer deployments at the risk of failure. At the same time, some early adopters were gaining valuable insights and benefits from the deployment of this technology. We asked ourselves how a company looking at understanding and implementing this technology could make an informed decision and take action. This book should provide the answer.

This book is not a theoretical treatise on competitive advantage—although it does point out examples of how companies can gain competitive advantage from RFID deployments; nor is it a technical manual providing code samples—although it does go into detailed technical discussion of the fundamentals of RFID. This book is a *field guide* for the practitioner.

A practitioner could be a business person, a technical person, or a person wearing both hats. It could be a senior executive trying to separate reality from the hype surrounding RFID and wondering if this technology can give him a leg up on the competition. Or, it could be a plant manager trying to figure out sourcing and production issues involved in applying RFID tags to an item in production. In this book, each of these practitioners will find real-life examples of RFID deployments relevant to their needs; issues related to people, processes, and technology; and tips for making an RFID deployment successful.

The book is organized into three parts. The first part explains RFID technology by providing its history, its components, and a perspective on what it can do for you. Because no technology can succeed and proliferate unless it helps businesses meet one or more of their primary economic needs—reducing cost, increasing revenue, and providing a competitive advantage—we also provide examples of RFID usage and its benefits to businesses and end users.

The second part explains how you can deploy RFID in your organization. RFID standards, an RFID analysis and deployment framework, cost-benefit considerations, and RFID vendor considerations are explained here. It outlines a holistic approach to doing an RFID project that can harness this complex technology for achieving real business benefits. You may think that putting an RFID tag on a box is not a complex task (which, by the way, is true—it takes only 10 seconds for an assembly worker to put a tag on a box and pass it along, an activity known as *slap & ship*). However, unless the process has been thought through, you are not likely to see much benefit from tagging an item. The challenge is not in applying the tag to an item, but in rethinking existing business processes or creating new ones to fully leverage the powerful, real-time data collection capability offered by RFID. RFID also brings with it a new set of challenges—for example, how to process all the data generated by billions of tags in the supply chain, how to filter the processed data, and how to integrate the filtered data into existing systems and processes to increase benefits. The framework and tools we provide in the second part help you think through such issues pertinent to your environment.

The third part looks at the path ahead. It explains how external factors such as mandates, legislation, regulations, political interest, and consumer concerns such as security and privacy can affect a technology's proliferation. It also provides a high-level view of the trends surrounding RFID deployments—from trends in tag design to invention of new business models.

The book is designed to cater to various types of practitioners. Some may be interested in reading the whole book first to get a comprehensive understanding of the technology. Others may simply want answers to their specific questions. To balance the needs of both types of readers, we have put in a section at the beginning of each chapter titled "Five Questions This Chapter Will Answer." Advanced readers will find these questions quite useful in determining the type of information covered in each chapter. For example, do you want to find out about the different types of tags and the frequencies they operate at? Turn to Chapter 3. Confused about the differences in RFID standards between the U.S., Europe, and China? Turn to Chapter 4 for clarification. Tasked with developing a business case for RFID? Turn to Chapter 7 for discussion of short-term and long-term benefits of RFID and advice on developing a cost-benefit analysis. Want to learn about the emerging trends in RFID? You will like the discussion in Chapter 11. The companion Web site for this book (*www.rfidfieldguide.com*) provides further pertinent information such as analysis of more than 250 vendors.

While our names appear on the cover, a project of this magnitude almost always involves a larger team: a team consisting of customers, vendors, editors, and reviewers. Without their generous help, support, and suggestions, this book would have remained only in concept. The virtual team members are too many to mention, but a few deserve special credit. We would like to thank the team at our publishers, Prentice Hall and Sun Microsystems Press, for their tireless efforts in getting the book in its current format: Greg Doench, Jennifer Blackwell, Stephane Nakib, Michael Thurston, Jill Tomich, Kelli Brooks, Matt Thompson, Myrna Rivera, and Jennifer Kohnke. We would also like to thank the reviewers for taking the time to review the book: Bill Camarda, Sanjay Sharma, and Bob Ganley. Special thanks to Angela Chen, Jim Clarke, Eli Covert, Soad Farhoud, Sandy Frye, Robert Fourdraine, Kevin Kirk, Stephen Lambright, Kijoon Lee, Michael Liard, Fred Nadel, Paula Phelan, Stephen Philpy, Jerry Proc, Vijay Sarathy, Scott Stuart, Jens Voges, Karen deVries, and Jihye Wang for their contributions and help with our research. During the course of this book, we conducted many interviews with customers and industry practitioners. Their insights and knowledge around real-world issues surrounding RFID deployments have been instrumental in making this book a *field guide*. We couldn't have created this field guide without their generosity. To them, we extend our most sincere gratitude.

We hope that you walk away from this book with a better appreciation for the technology as well as a practical understanding of how to make RFID work in your business.

Shahram Moradpour • *Manish Bhuptani*

PART I

WHAT IS RFID?

1

A Better Way of Doing Things

Five Questions This Chapter Will Answer

- How is RFID used in my industry/business?
- What makes RFID so "hot" in the supply chain industry?
- Can people really put RFID tags under their skin?
- Isn't RFID technology just a more sophisticated form of barcode technology?
- When will RFID be widely deployed?

The invention of the wheel is considered one of the most significant discoveries of all time—not because of what the wheel can do in isolation, but because of the many ways it can be harnessed to reduce friction between objects and surfaces. Wheelbarrows, wagons, bicycles, cars, and airplanes outline a progression of contemporary uses, 8,500 years after early potter's grokked the "cool factor." These well-known applications for the wheel make life better and easier for all of us but they scratch the surface in describing the myriad of ways in which the wheel is now employed. In much the same way, but in a significantly more accelerated fashion, the invention of Radio Frequency Identification (RFID) technology is following a parallel path in becoming a ubiquitous enabler for doing things better than we used to.

In a typical RFID system, described in detail in Chapter 3, "Components of RFID Systems," objects are tagged with tiny radio transponders that carry certain data about the objects. The transponders (tags) transmit this data, through radio waves, to nearby readers, which collect and process the data accordingly. These transactions between RFID tags and readers enable a multitude of applications that require efficient detection, identification, and tracking of objects. Although many RFID-enabled applications already exist today, it is expected that RFID will be used in a dramatically growing number of applications over the next five years. According to Venture Development Corporation, a technology market research firm, global shipments of RFID systems are expected to grow at a 45.6% compounded annual growth rate (CAGR), from $1.5 billion in 2004 to $4.7 billion in 2007[1]. Separately, ABI Research reports that an expected 12.3 billion RFID tags will be shipped in 2008, up from an estimated 365 million in 2003[2].

In this chapter, we offer a snapshot of the various ways that RFID applications help us do things in a better way. These applications are categorized and described in terms of the major benefits they provide, which include the following:

- Security and authentication

- Safety

- Convenience

- Process efficiency

---

[1] Source: Venture Development Corporation. Used by permission.

[2] Source: ABI Research. Used by permission.

This approach will benefit you in the following ways:

- Enable you to get a deeper appreciation of RFID's capabilities
- Help you visualize the benefits of RFID in a vast array of businesses

We have drawn our examples from real-life applications that either have been deployed or are currently in development. There are cases, as summarized in Table 1.1, in which an RFID application provides more than one of these benefits. For example, the electronic drug pedigree application has a *primary* benefit of verifying and validating a medicine's origin (authentication), but it also has the *added* benefit of protecting the consumer (safety). However, in the sections that follow, we will only provide the description of each application in relation to its *primary* benefit.

Table 1.1 Typical RFID Applications and Their Benefits

Application	Benefits
EAS	Security and Authentication, Convenience
Document Authentication	Security and Authentication
Access Control	Security and Authentication, Safety
Electronic Drug Pedigree	Security and Authentication, Safety
People Monitoring	Safety, Process Efficiency

Table 1.1   continued

Application	Benefits
Patient Monitoring	Safety, Process Efficiency
Environment Sensing and Monitoring	Safety
Payment and Loyalty	Convenience, Process Efficiency
Crowd Control	Convenience, Process Efficiency, Security
Sports Timing	Convenience, Process Efficiency
Golf	Convenience, Process Efficiency
Track and Trace	Process Efficiency, Security and Authentication
Industrial Automation	Process Efficiency
Supply Chain Integration	Process Efficiency

Security and Authentication

One of the earliest uses of RFID has been in the area of security and authentication. The capability to identify, often uniquely, an object, a person, or an animal is achieved very simply with RFID tags. Some of the most popular uses of RFID in security and authentication include electronic article surveillance (EAS), document authentication, and electronic drug pedigree applications.

Electronic Article Surveillance (EAS)

What is it?

EAS, as illustrated in Figure 1.1, is one of the most basic applications of RFID for security. Objects such as articles of clothing are tagged with very inexpensive "1-bit" tags. The tags do not uniquely identify the objects but cause an alarm to go off or a camera to take a picture when an object moves within the range of specially situated readers.

FIGURE 1.1   A Typical Electronic Article Surveillance (EAS) Application

A new category of EAS solutions using sophisticated tags is gaining momentum. In these applications, tags are placed "into" products during their manufacture, thereby creating self-authenticating products with significantly lower risk of tampering, fraud, or counterfeiting. These product authentication tags are more costly and are generally used for expensive items such as designer brand clothing or medicine bottles.

Why use it?

Shoplifting costs retailers around the world billions of dollars every year. EAS systems can greatly reduce inventory shrinkage due to theft in retail and warehouse operations. Additionally, the likelihood of a stock-out (an item that goes unexpectedly out of stock) from shoplifting can be greatly reduced. Stock-outs can be very costly to both the retailer and the manufacturer. When faced with a stock-out, a customer might decide to buy a similar product from an alternate manufacturer or simply go to another store and buy the same product there. In either case, customer loyalty is jeopardized.

Document Authentication

What is it?

Document authentication is a new area for the use of RFID. It employs tags that uniquely identify and confirm the authenticity of the documents to which they are affixed. In January of 2004, the invitations to the Golden Globe Award ceremonies carried an inconspicuously embedded RFID tag, which reduced the possibility of counterfeiting, increased overall security, and enabled faster and easier movement and access for the participants. Other sophisticated applications use RFID to authenticate important items ranging from package deliveries and passports to identification cards and even currency.

Why use it?

Document authentication can detect and prevent fraud in addition to providing anti-counterfeiting measures. These benefits extend well beyond everyday enterprise or consumer use. We can expect this technology to be further deployed in various government and military applications.

Access Control

What is it?

RFID tags embedded in cards, key chains, or other similar carriers provide access control for any secure area such as an office building, a parking garage, or a car. Tags can be programmed to uniquely identify the holder of the tag, thereby allowing for a very granular authentication method by the reader. For example, a certain employee may be granted access to the lobby of an office building and certain designated offices. The same employee may be denied access to the computer server room or a secure storage area.

Why use it?

Access control RFID tags are a very cost effective and convenient method of providing secure, authenticated access. The tags cannot be easily duplicated or unintentionally destroyed or disabled. Additionally, access control rules programmed into the reader can easily be modified without the need to re-program the tag itself.

Electronic Drug Pedigree

What is it?

Vulnerability in the supply chain of drugs is a major issue for both pharmaceutical manufacturers and suppliers. There are many stops in the supply chain that represent a potential vulnerability, from secondary or foreign wholesalers to repackagers and Internet pharmacies. RFID technology can be used to tag drug packages and essentially build and record their pedigree as they move through different links in the supply chain.

Why use it?

Counterfeit drugs not only cause monetary damage to the manufacturers, but, more importantly, they pose a potential health risk to the consumer. Counterfeit drugs can be made using lower standards or having poor quality. They may indeed have no active ingredients at all. Some may even contain the wrong ingredients. Electronic drug pedigree methods can help to secure and authenticate drugs shipped by manufacturers and reduce the risk of tampering and counterfeiting. This use of RFID technology offers the capability to trace a drug's pedigree as it moves through numerous links in the supply chain. Additionally, the capability to monitor and record data at every stop in the supply chain helps isolate the source of counterfeiting activity in the chain.

Safety

In general, members of a modern society develop personal attachments and endeavor to ensure the safety of people close to them. In the business world, there are monetary benefits associated with providing safe environments for employees and customers. For example, a hospital can secure lower malpractice insurance rates if it can demonstrate a decrease in the number of cases where patients receive the wrong medication. A number of applications use RFID technology to help create safer working conditions and environments while also providing peace of mind. Some of the popular ones are outlined here.

People Monitoring

What is it?

The capability to know a person's whereabouts and monitor his or her movements has a number of significant benefits. Although unauthorized people monitoring can be a violation of privacy rights, there are several applications of consented monitoring, especially for seniors, which can be helpful and potentially life saving.

Some amusement parks around the world offer a service allowing parents to track their children and pinpoint their location using RFID bracelets. For an illustration of this application, see Figure 1.2. In one instance, children are outfitted with active RFID bracelets that can be tracked by strategically located readers throughout the park. The parents are also outfitted with corresponding RFID tags. Monitoring stations allow parents to validate their identity using their RFID tags and then give them exclusive permission to locate only their child. After the child's location is identified in the park, strategically located cameras zoom in to reveal the child's precise location and status.

In yet another application, the location and movement of elderly or disabled persons can be monitored and acted upon. For example, to ensure that Alzheimer's patients living in a care facility do not leave their rooms without keys, door handles can be outfitted with RFID readers that can detect the absence of an RFID tagged room key and alert the patient and/or a caregiver via any combination of alarm types.

Why use it?

The two significant benefits of tracking potentially vulnerable loved ones revolve around real-time safety and on-demand peace of mind. Additionally, the capability to monitor the whereabouts and movements of children, elderly, or disabled persons can save a considerable amount of time and money by reducing the amount of dedicated personal care that might otherwise be required.

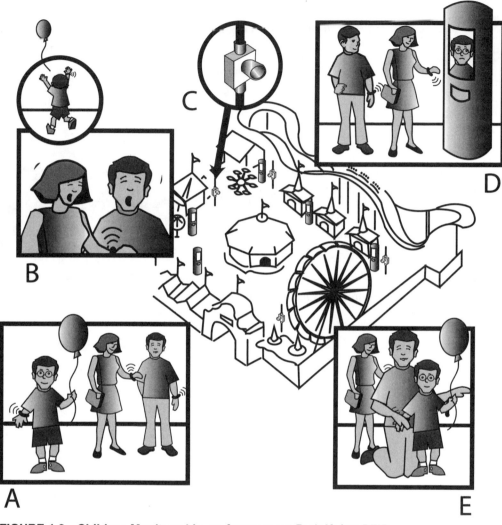

FIGURE 1.2   Children Monitored in an Amusement Park Using RFID

Patient Care

What is it?

RFID can create a safer and more comfortable environment for hospital patients in many different ways. One of the more common uses is to put RFID tagged bracelets on newborns in the maternity ward to ensure they are always matched with their mothers and that they are not being transported off the premises without authorization. An audible alarm is activated if the RFID bracelet is cut, as if to be removed without authorization.

Bracelet tagging can have more sophisticated uses that can uniquely identify a patient and her prescribed medication. This *mobile patient database* can contain additional information such as a patient's blood type, allergies, and other important health information. New data that might include vital statistics or the date of last physician visit can be written onto the tag in real-time, thereby giving doctors and nurses instant and accurate access to patient data. See Figure 1.3 for an illustrative example of this application.

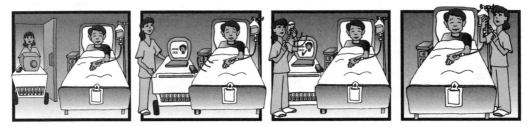

FIGURE 1.3   A Patient-Monitoring Application Using RFID

Why use it?

Patient health, safety, and comfort are major concerns for hospitals. Although physicians, nurses, and other staff take primary responsibility for safety, RFID technology enables a more efficient care process. Simultaneously, it increases patient satisfaction while decreasing possibilities for errors caused by the "separation" of information from a patient. Apart from the obvious benefits of patient safety and good reputation, decreased patient/data error rates can help to reduce malpractice claims and industry insurance rates.

Environment Sensing and Monitoring

What is it?

RFID technology can be integrated with devices that sense and monitor various environmental conditions. Poultry and other meat-related supply chains always present a challenge for the accurate monitoring of temperature ranges. These perishables must be closely monitored to ensure that spoilage does not occur. RFID technology addresses this challenge with specially outfitted temperature sensors that are applied to meat packaging to monitor temperatures at all times. The sensors can be programmed to detect, record, and alert others about any breach of a predefined temperature threshold. The same technology can be used in clinical settings to monitor the temperature of donated blood and body organs during transport. Safety benefits could also result from RFID tags with bacterial sensors that measure and report data regarding potential contamination of food products.

Another area where sensing devices provide useful functionality is tamper detection of safety-critical products such as non-prescription drugs and cosmetics. Special sensors with RFID tags can detect and record any package that has been tampered with. This allows tamper checking of multiple packages of the product that may be contained in sealed cases or pallets while sidestepping time-consuming, and thus costly, processes of checking each individual item. Additionally, the integrity of the product can be monitored as it moves through the supply chain to help isolate and identify possible tampering sources.

Sensing devices are also integrated with RFID technology to monitor and report tire pressure in vehicles. An air pressure sensor monitors and records the tire pressure on an RFID tag, which can then be queried by the car's onboard reader and any irregularities reported to the driver through the vehicle's dashboard instrumentation. See Figure 1.4 for an illustrative example of this application.

FIGURE 1.4 Tire Pressure Monitoring Using RFID

Why use it?

Sensors with RFID technology are fast becoming a common tool to help measure and report various environmental conditions that affect our everyday lives. Monitoring and exception reporting has several advantages. For the consumer, it creates unprecedented peace of mind given an immense number of changing environmental variables that can pose safety risks in our daily lives. For the business, it provides a better safety control mechanism with the added benefits of lowering the risk of liability and increasing customer satisfaction and confidence.

Convenience

RFID-enabled services or applications designed to bring greater convenience for the consumer usually create a more efficient process for the provider of the service or application, thereby helping to reduce cost. In other words, providing the benefit of convenience to the consumer provides an eventual cost reduction to the provider, thus answering the "Why use it?" question, which we posed separately in the previous sections. To avoid redundancy, we have eliminated the structural division between "What is it?" and "Why use it?" in this section.

Payment and Loyalty

RFID payment and loyalty cards represent a convenient means for consumers to pay for purchased goods. Obtaining and placing an electronic toll collection payment tag on a vehicle's dashboard enables a customer to navigate toll roads, bridges, and tunnels more efficiently.

An RFID enabled key chain at a gas station speeds up the fuel purchasing process by facilitating a "contact-less" billing transaction. Payment tags also provide additional convenience benefits when used, invisibly, to pay for public transportation services or for vending machine products. The primary source of convenience is the contact-less feature of RFID, thus eliminating difficulties with finding change or credit cards and reducing, if not eliminating, inconvenient waiting lines.

Crowd Control

Use of RFID tags to ensure that patrons have paid for and are entitled to certain services and privileges is quite common. Examples include RFID tagged tickets at ski resorts or sports stadiums that do not require physical (that is, barcode) or visual inspection. Such tags can usually be combined with the payment tag feature that allows the consumer to also buy food or other goods through a pre-paid account in a convenient, contact-less manner.

These consumer benefits not only bring more accuracy and efficiency for a business, but they also build loyalty. Additionally, the convenience factor may also lead consumers to purchase more goods and services than they might have otherwise.

Recently, some VIP members at the Baja Beach Club in Barcelona have reportedly taken RFID technology to a sub-dermal level. Instead of carrying a typical card, members may opt to "get chipped"—a procedure involving a local anesthetic followed immediately with a chip injection under the skin of one's upper left arm, near the triceps. Not only does the chip enable VIPs to jump entrance lines more quickly, but it also functions as an in-house debit card, which enables paperless tallying and payment of one's tab.

Sports Timing

RFID tags provide a very convenient and accurate way to measure participants' time in sporting events. This application has gained popularity in only a few years and will likely continue the momentum as the cost of RFID components goes down and the technology becomes more economically viable.

Golf Ball Tracking

Because golf is one of our favorite hobbies, we discuss it briefly. There are two handy applications, one for the golf course and one for the driving range. The first, illustrated in Figure 1.5, involves tracking lost golf balls. An RFID tag, embedded inside a golf ball, can be tracked and found using a handheld reader. This not only has the benefit of speeding up play and minimizing stroke penalties, but it also saves money by reducing the number of lost golf balls. The second application offers the capability to measure the distance that a golf ball has traveled at the driving range by using RFID tagged golf balls. These tagged balls are detected by strategically located readers around the range.

FIGURE 1.5 Tracking a Lost Golf Ball Using RFID

Process Efficiency

Businesses are always looking for ways to improve their cost structure. One way to reduce overhead is to streamline various operational processes. For continuous fine-tuning, accurate and effective measurement of process efficiency is crucial. RFID-enabled applications can offer the monitoring capability to vastly improve upon a wide range of processes. Because RFID technologies can electronically capture data during certain steps in a process, data about operational results becomes more readily available in real-time. This, in turn, facilitates a more insightful analysis and adjustment of operational processes. Here, we discuss some of the more common applications of RFID that can bring process efficiency gains to business operations.

Track and Trace

What is it?

Tracking and tracing objects is one of the most common applications of RFID to help improve process efficiency and reduce overhead costs. An outline of some of the more common applications is shown in the following sections.

Inventory Control   Automated tracking devices for inventory control in factories and warehouses have the primary advantage of lowering costs by reducing the amount of manual work and operations. There are certainly other means of achieving automated tracking, besides RFID. The most common is barcode technology. However, there are several major advantages that RFID technology offers beyond barcodes:

- RFID requires no line of sight. RFID tags can be read, at much greater speeds than barcodes, regardless of the orientation or placement with respect to the reader.

- Depending on the underlying RFID technology, much longer read ranges of up to several feet or more can be achieved, compared to a barcode's read range, which is typically measured in inches.

- Barcodes are a read-only medium. RFID tags with write capability offer an added benefit of acting as small, mobile databases that can store data at will, instantly.

- Barcodes can be destroyed easily or removed and cannot readily be applied to all substrates like skin or clothing.

Figure 1.6 depicts a simple packaged goods factory scenario where many tracking and tracing steps traditionally done through manual or barcode systems can be RFID enabled to gain more efficiency and visibility into factory and warehouse operations.

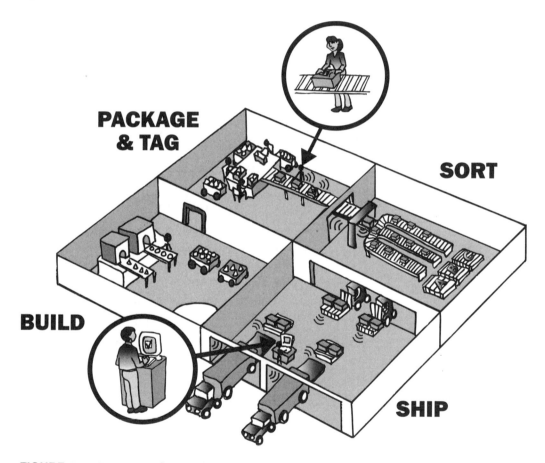

FIGURE 1.6   Packaged Goods Track and Trace Operations Using RFID

Luggage Tracking   Luggage tracking with RFID technology can help achieve several time-saving objectives. RFID tags can be applied to luggage at passenger check-in time. This allows for a more efficient sorting and routing of luggage as it moves down the conveyor belt, which is outfitted with strategically placed RFID readers, which control the conveyor belt's automated routing mechanism. RFID tags minimize the requirement for manual operations, thereby improving speed and accuracy of routing. Because RFID tags do not require line-of-sight visibility to RFID readers, luggage does not have to be reoriented or handled in order to be read. After check-in, suspicious luggage can be tagged and routed to a secondary inspection spot. After inspection, the RFID tag on the luggage will ensure quick and efficient return of the luggage to its destination bin with minimal manual intervention.

Document Tracking   Tracking of important documents, such as patient files at a hospital or client files at a law office or an insurance company, can increase the speed and accuracy of retrieval and reduce the risk of lost files due to inadvertent misfiling. The label used to tag a document carries a history log of authorized users and even a handling trail. This helps to create a more useful and secure workflow history.

Rental Item Processing   Long lines at libraries, video stores, and other rental stores are a deterrent to potential consumers. The use of RFID systems can greatly increase the speed of checkout and return. By reducing waiting, customer satisfaction improves, plus a smaller staff can easily administer a larger workload.

Asset Management   Any asset in a business or a home can be tracked and managed with RFID tags. The decision of whether to track an item using an RFID tag relates directly to its value, whether monetary or utilitarian. A diverse group of items that have been tagged and tracked includes the following:

- Books
- Sports memorabilia
- Easily misplaced household items
- Laundry at the dry cleaners
- Cafeteria trays
- Beer kegs
- Railroad cars
- Casino slot machine keys

Smart Shelves The Smart Shelves application involves the capability to detect tagged items on shelves through a series of strategically placed readers and antennae on and around the shelves. The idea is to detect when an item is removed or added to a shelf—for example, to enforce better inventory control or monitor sales. Smart Shelves are most commonly used to track high value items such as surgical instruments in hospitals. Wide use and deployment of Smart Shelves is directly dependent on the cost of implementation. In this case, the cost of the tag taken as a percentage of the item cost will play a large role in determining the application's viability. If the inventory is not valuable enough, as with packages of candy, the application may not be economically viable. The cost of installation of new and custom RFID-enabled shelving infrastructure can also play a significant role in determining viability. Today, several pilots are being considered to build Smart Shelves in retail stores for tracking ordinary items such as groceries or clothing. However, due to the aforementioned cost considerations, retail Smart Shelves are not expected to be widely deployed for several more years.

Why use it?

Using RFID to track objects in and of itself is beneficial because it enables greater process efficiency and reduces errors, overhead, and cost. However, the task of tagging and tracking an item in a supply chain is the first and most critical step in helping to create a more efficient integrated supply chain, discussed shortly.

Industrial Automation

What is it?

Use of RFID in industrial automation is commonplace. On the manufacturing floor, whether automotive equipment, disk drives, computers, or machinery, an item may be subject to hundreds of steps from the start of processing to finished product. RFID tags are used to help reduce the overhead and errors associated with moving through such stepwise progression. Because every step must be preceded by another specific and predetermined step, RFID tags are used to record the steps an item has gone through. At each new step, a reader queries the tag to ensure that the item has undergone all previously required steps before going through the current one. This is most helpful when a product goes through a process that forever changes its appearance, as in repainting. For example, when an automobile part gets to a new step on the assembly line, the process may call for a treatment that depends on an original

color that is no longer visible. An embedded or strategically placed RFID tag, however, reports on what the original color was and allows the application of the correct
treatment at this new step.

Why use it?

RFID technology on the factory floor or in an automated assembly line is a time-
saving process that reduces manual labor and human error. It is often the only
effective way to positively identify objects that are subjected to various treatments
such as extreme heat, mechanical force, or color change that dramatically change
their appearance.

Supply Chain Integration

What is it?

Supply chain integration is essentially the most extended application of tracking and
tracing. It encompasses the tracking of literally anything in a supply chain, including
raw materials from various suppliers, to manufacturing, and all the way to final delivery of a product to the end user. In the supply chain, there are numerous, seemingly
unrelated, business entities involved in processes that get the item to the next link in
the supply chain, closer to the end user. Capturing and integrating data about the
location and history of an item in the supply chain can help create more efficient
workflow and error-free processes. RFID technology is an ideal enabler to help track
the movement of products through the links in the supply chain, inspect and analyze
the data collected from RFID tags, act upon the data, and potentially add or associate more useful data to the tags that can be used at the next link in the chain.

The number of businesses that may touch a supply chain and the large number
of processes that can be RFID enabled make the application and deployment of an
end-to-end RFID-enabled supply chain solution potentially daunting. The Smart and
Secure Tradelanes case study in Appendix A demonstrates this complexity. In this
very large commercial supply chain initiative, there are 65 participants across three
continents monitoring 818 shipping containers through 18 tradelanes. This multi-
phase project began in July 2002 and is expected to continue for several years before
it is complete.

The catalysts that are driving RFID adoption into the supply chain are recent
mandates from the United States Department of Defense (DoD), Wal-Mart, and
other retailers, along with more favorable prices of RFID components, particularly

tags. Although most of today's RFID-enabled supply chain solutions look at applying RFID between only two points (only one link) in the chain, fully integrating the links in the supply chain is recognized as the real value liberator. The more processes in the supply chain that can be integrated through RFID-collected data, the greater the potential for improvement in efficiency. This is the ultimate power of RFID. Sourcing and procurement, packaging, distribution, inventory control, forecasting, transportation, and logistics are all processes common to many supply chain operations. Linking these up to all the businesses and integrating all the processes in the supply chain is the challenge for the next decade.

A word of caution here is in order. Although RFID is a natural enabler for supply chain integration, several intermediate issues must be addressed before RFID can realize its full potential in the supply chain. These issues are introduced here briefly and discussed in more detail in Chapter 4, "Standards Related to RFID," and Chapter 5, "Framework for Deployment."

- **Serialization (unique identification):** Most supply chain processes and applications are designed today to work with barcode technology. As such, they do not have a concept of a *unique identifier* for each instance of a product/item (barcodes can only identify a class of items such as a particular brand and size of cereal box). As a result, business processes and their associated software applications will have to be redesigned to address the concept of unique identifiers before they can fully benefit from an RFID-enabled system.

- **Data synchronization:** Data synchronization involves the complete, accurate, and timely updating and reporting of product/item data exchanged between trading partners in a supply chain. Historically, this has been an issue between trading partners such as consumer packaged goods manufacturers and their retail counterparts. Although data synchronization is not an RFID issue *per se*, it is nevertheless a critical issue to be resolved, especially since RFID can worsen the situation because it can potentially generate more inaccurate data and make it more readily available.

- **Standardization:** Supply chain integration, by definition, requires cooperation and communication between a diverse set of hardware components and software applications and among many different trading partners. Standardization is the only effective means of satisfying this requirement in an efficient and cost effective fashion. Additionally, both serialization and data synchronization can largely be addressed through adherence to standards. Standardization is such a critical topic that we have dedicated an entire chapter (Chapter 4) to it.

Why use it?

Supply chain integration is expected, by analysts, businesses, and vendors alike, to become one of the most widely used applications of RFID. Process efficiency resulting from improving visibility in the supply chain of anything from packaged goods to farm animals brings about cost savings to more than one business because there are potentially dozens of businesses involved in the handling of goods through a supply chain. Ultimately, these cost savings can be translated into benefits that positively affect the end user/consumer and as a result an entire industry—for example, retail—as a whole.

Summary

The ubiquitous adoption of RFID technology is well underway. There were already more than one billion tags in use by the end of the year 2004. We expect this number to increase by several tens of billions before the end of the decade.

We use RFID technology when we enter our office buildings or when we go shopping for a favorite pair of shoes. We use it in our golf courses and in marathon races. It enables us to secure our vehicles and navigate toll ways quickly. RFID tags help to prevent food and even blood or donor organs from inadvertent spoilage, and they ensure higher levels of safety and accuracy when matching hospital patients with relevant medical data. In certain scenarios, RFID technologies help locate and protect loved ones. In the not too distant future, RFID technology may prevent a gun from being fired by anyone other than its licensed owner.

The next wave for RFID ubiquity is expected to come from its adoption in the supply chain. Deploying RFID-enabled solutions that help integrate the entire supply chain, from manufacturing at the raw material level all the way into the hands of the end user, promises process efficiencies, significant cost savings, and convenience to all parties involved throughout the supply chain. The journey will take time because the economics are still evolving and improving, and the value proposition to businesses is complex to articulate and implement. We start in the next chapter by outlining the history of RFID to give you a better sense of how far the technology has come since it was first used during World War II.

2

THE HISTORY AND EVOLUTION OF RFID

Five Questions This Chapter Will Answer

- When and why was RFID invented?
- What major milestones have been achieved in the development of RFID applications?
- Who are some of the earliest RFID market makers?
- When did the application of RFID in supply chain become reality?
- Why was EPCglobal established?

A review of the evolution of RFID technology and its components will help you visualize and better realize the full potential of the applications of RFID technology today and in the near future. This chapter will provide the following:

- A historical account of RFID's evolution and the major milestones to date

- A sneak peek at the benefits RFID's eventual ubiquity will bring to consumers and businesses alike

RFID Technology and the Radio

Although the history of RFID can be traced to the 1930s, the technology underlying RFID finds its roots back in 1897, when Guglielmo Marconi invented the radio. RFID applies the same principles of physics as those used in radio broadcasting, where radio waves, a form of electromagnetic energy, transmit and receive various types of data.

To better understand this similarity, visualize a radio station broadcasting voice or music through a transmitter. This is essentially data encoded into radio waves of a specific frequency. In a separate location, the listener has a radio that can be tuned to decode the data (voice or music) being transmitted by the radio station. Almost everyone has experienced the changes in quality of radio reception when traveling by car. The further you get from the transmitter, the weaker the signal becomes. The distance in all directions, or area, that a radio transmission can cover is determined by environmental conditions and the size and power of the antennae on each side of the communication link. Using RFID terminology, the radio station transmitter functions like a *tag*, also known as the *transponder* (derived from the terms *trans*mitter and res*ponder*), while the radio is the *reader*, also known as the *interrogator*. The *antennae* determine the reach, also known as the *range*.

These three components—the transponder or the tag, the receiver or the reader, and the antennae—are the building blocks of all RFID systems. Variations in power, size, antenna design, operating frequency, data capacity, and software to manage and interpret the data create a myriad of possible applications where RFID technology can be used to solve real-world business problems.

The Early Days of RFID

In the 1930s, both the Army and the Navy were faced with the challenge of adequately identifying targets on the ground, at sea and in the air. In 1937, the U.S. Naval Research Laboratory (NRL) developed the Identification Friend-or-Foe (IFF) system that allowed friendly units such as Allied aircraft to be distinguished from enemy aircraft. This technology became the basis for the world's air traffic control systems beginning in the late 1950s. Early uses of radio identification through the 1950s were generally limited to the military, research labs, and large commercial enterprises because of the high cost and large size of components. Even so, these expensive and bulky equipment racks were the early forerunners of what is now called RFID. Figure 2.1 shows photos of IFF components next to typical modern day RFID components[1].

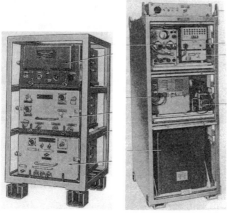

242 Interrogator   **253 Transponder**   **Savi Fixed Reader**   **SaviTag ST-654,**
                                                     SR-650, Interrogator   **Transponder**

Interrogator and Transponder stand several feet tall.   Active tag weighs less than 4 ounces.
Photos Courtesy of The British Admiralty   Reader weighs 4 pounds.
Reproduced from a paper by Jerry Proc   Photos Courtesy of Savi Technology

FIGURE 2.1   IFF Components (left), Modern Day (Active) RFID Components (right)

It was not until the emergence of more compact and cost-effective technologies such as the integrated circuit (IC), programmable memory chips, the microprocessor, and modern day software applications and programming languages that RFID as we know it today was born and moved into the mainstream of broad commercial deployment.

---

[1] The modern day RFID components shown in Figure 2.1 are not equivalent in capability and functionality to the IFF components and are used for different types of applications.

During the late 1960s and early 1970s, companies such as Sensormatic and Checkpoint Systems introduced new uses of RFID for less complex and more widely used applications. These companies began developing electronic article surveillance (EAS) equipment to protect inventory items such as clothing in department stores and books in libraries. Early commercial RFID systems, also known as 1-bit tag systems, were inexpensive to build, deploy, and maintain. Tags required no battery power (passive) and were simply affixed to articles that were designed to trigger an alarm when they came near a reader, usually at an exit door, which would detect the presence of a tag.

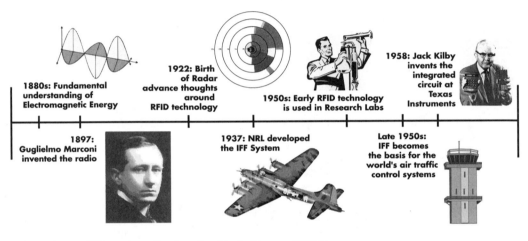

FIGURE 2.2   Milestones During the Early Days of RFID

From Detection to Unique Identification

During the 1970s, industries such as manufacturing, livestock, and transportation commenced research and development projects to find ways to use IC-based RFID systems. Applications like industrial automation, animal identification, and vehicle tracking were all under consideration. During this period, IC-based tags continued to advance and featured writeable memory, faster read speeds, and longer ranges. Many of these RFID applications were based on proprietary designs and did not leverage the power of a standards-based approach.

In the early 1980s, more sophisticated RFID technologies were employed in applications ranging from identification of railroad cars in the United States to tracking farm animals in Europe. RFID systems were also used in wildlife studies to tag and track exotic or endangered species such as fish with minimal intrusion into their natural habitats.

In the 1990s, electronic toll collection systems gained popularity on both sides of the Atlantic, with commercial implementations in Italy, France, Spain, Portugal, Norway, and in the United States in Dallas, New York, and New Jersey. These systems offered a more sophisticated form of access control because they also included a payment mechanism.

Starting in 1990, several regional toll agencies in the northeastern United States joined forces under the name of E-ZPass Interagency Group (IAG), and together they developed a regionally compatible electronic toll collection system. This step was a major milestone toward creating application-level standards for interoperability. Until this point, most standardization efforts were centered on technical attributes such as frequency of operation and hardware communication protocols.

E-ZPass enabled a single tag to correspond to a single billing account per vehicle. The tagged vehicle then had access to highways of multiple toll authorities without having to stop at a tollbooth. E-Z Pass helped traffic to flow more easily and dramatically reduced the labor involved in collecting tolls and handling cash.

Around the same time, RFID card keys became increasingly popular as a replacement for traditional access control mechanisms such as metallic keys and combination locks. These so-called contactless smart cards provided information about the user and thus offered a more personalized method of access control, while being inexpensive to produce and program. Table 2.1 compares the most common methods of access control with that of RFID access control.

TABLE 2.1   Comparison of Various Access Control Methods

Access Control Method	Pros	Cons
Metallic Key	• Does not need electricity to function • Easy to use	• Can be copied easily • Lock can be picked • Susceptible to theft
Combination Lock	• Combination can be easily changed • No key to be lost or stolen	• More expensive than a key-lock • Vulnerable to eavesdropping
Punch Card	• Cannot be duplicated as easily as a metallic key	• Older technology with little flexibility • Easy to duplicate
Magnetic Strip	• Cannot be easily copied • Card readers widely available	• Prolonged use can damage card • Installation requires costly IT infrastructure
Smart Card	• Same card can also be used for applications other than access control (e.g. payment) • Provides more security than Magnetic Strip Cards	• More expensive than a Magnetic Strip Card
RFID	• All the Pros of Smart Cards • Requires no contact • Can be embedded in items other than cards and under the skin	• Can be more expensive than Smart Cards

RFID access control has continued to gain new levels of acceptance. Automobile manufacturers have been using RFID tags for nearly a decade to control the ignition systems in their vehicles, resulting in dramatic reductions in car theft. Most recently, some automakers have equipped their vehicles with RFID systems that directly control entry into the passenger compartment and the trunk.

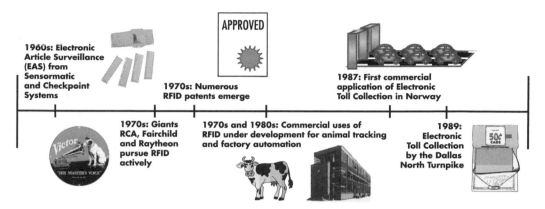

FIGURE 2.3   Milestones from the 1960s to the 1990s

RFID Flourishes Across the Globe

By the end of the twentieth century, the number of modern RFID applications began to expand exponentially across the globe. Here we examine a few of the significant developments that conributed to this accelerated rate of adoption.

Texas Instruments Leads Pioneering Efforts in the U.S.

Texas Instruments pioneered modern RFID systems in the United States when, in 1991, the company created the Texas Instruments Registration and Identification Systems (TIRIS). Known today as TI-RFid (Texas Instruments Radio Frequency Identification System), it has become a vibrant platform for developing and implementing dozens of new classes of RFID applications.

Europe Gets an Early Start

Even before Texas Instruments made its presence known in RFID, pieces of the puzzle were coming together in Europe. Starting in the 1970s, EM Microelectronic-Marin (also known as EM-Marin)—a company of The Swatch Group Ltd.—designed miniaturized, ultra low-power integrated circuits for watches in Switzerland. In 1982, Mikron Integrated Microelectronics manufactured ASIC technology and, in 1987, added an Austrian subsidiary, mikron Graz, to develop technology specifically related to identification and smart card chips. Philips Semiconductors acquired mikron Graz in 1995. Today, both EM Microelectronic and Philips Semiconductors are two of the major players in European RFID efforts.

Passive Tags Grow Up in the '90s

Until just a few years ago, the majority of passive RFID applications, illustrated in Table 2.2, were deployed at the Low Frequency (LF) and High Frequency (HF) range of the RF spectrum. Both LF and HF systems have limitations in range and speed of data transmission. For practical purposes, the range for these systems can be measured in inches. The speed limitations prevent the reading of tags in applications where hundreds or even thousands of tags might be present in a reader's field at any given moment in time. It wasn't until the end of the 1990s when Ultra High Frequency (UHF) passive tags were able to offer the combination of better range, higher speed, and attractive pricing that passive tags were able to step beyond their original limitations. Because of these added features, UHF-based RFID systems became primary candidates for new uses in supply chain applications, including pallet and case tracking, inventory control, and warehouse and logistics management. We discuss the various attributes and applications of the different passive tag technologies in detail in Chapter 3, "Components of RFID Systems."

TABLE 2.2   Typical Applications Using Passive LF and HF RFID Technology

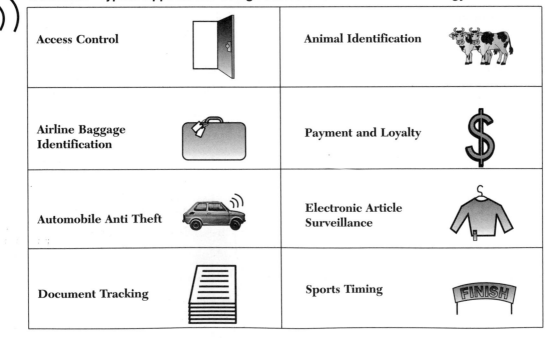

Access Control	**Animal Identification**
Airline Baggage Identification	**Payment and Loyalty**
Automobile Anti Theft	**Electronic Article Surveillance**
Document Tracking	**Sports Timing**

During the late 1990s and early 2000s, retailers such as Wal-Mart, Target, and Metro Group and government agencies such as the U.S. Department of Defense (DoD), started to promote and require the use of RFID by their suppliers. Around the same time, the industry-sponsored, non-profit consortium, EPCglobal was formed. EPCglobal supported the Electronic Product Code (EPC) Network, which became a de facto standard for automatic identification of items in the supply chains around the world. Thus, there was established for the first time, a global requirement for the deployment of RFID systems and a standards body ready to help facilitate the implementation of this requirement.

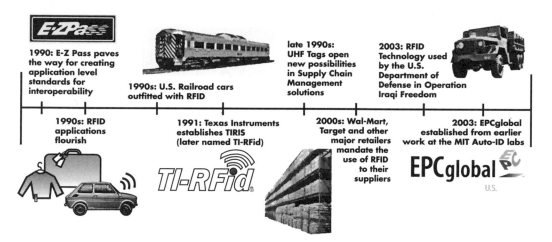

FIGURE 2.4   Milestones from the 1990s to Today

What is EPCglobal?

EPCglobal is a non-profit organization formed as a joint venture between EAN International and the Uniform Code Council (UCC) to support the Electronic Product Code (EPC) Network as the standard for automatic identification of items in the supply chain of companies around the world. EPCglobal has received sponsorship from more than one hundred of the world's leading companies, many of which are consumer household names such as Gillette and Procter and Gamble. The EPC and the EPCglobal Network are intended to help businesses improve asset visibility and help ensure product safety and integrity across the supply chain. The EPCglobal Network was initially developed by the Auto-ID Center, headquartered at the Massachusetts Institute of Technology (MIT) under Dr. Sanjay Sarma, Research Director of the Auto-ID Center. With three distinct action groups, EPCglobal is fully represented by the user community and focuses on hardware and software development and business requirements. You can read more about EPCglobal in Chapter 3, "Components of RFID Systems," and Chapter 4, "Standards Related to RFID."

Summary

Historians and technology pundits generally agree that it takes twenty to thirty years for a technology to become commercialized and often 40 to 50 years before it becomes fully mature. As with radio, television, the transistor, and the computer, RFID saw only modest use for the first thirty years after its inception. Then, after an extended incubation period, a groundswell occurred, which culminated in the full-blown commercialization of RFID and a corresponding change to the lives of millions of people around the globe. RFID is now at the precipice of another major evolution that will change and improve the lives of businesses and individuals everywhere.

History also illustrates that creative new uses of technologies such as RFID will continue to spring up as long as the demand or the economics of an implementation make sense. During wartime, IFF was indispensable after it became possible. Twenty years later, similar technologies were used in air traffic control systems. Today, convenience, economics, and the promise of interoperability will be the governing forces that drive the development and adoption of new RFID applications.

Although the underlying technology for RFID has existed since Marconi invented the radio at the turn of the twentieth century, we have only recently begun to tap into the full potential of RFID. The beginning of the twenty-first century marked a significant inflection point for RFID systems. We are now embarking on a new wave of innovation in the use of RFID systems that will drive it even further into the fabric of our everyday lives.

The remainder of the book discusses all the elements necessary to design and implement RFID-enabled applications successfully. In the next chapter, we start by providing a detailed description of the most common components used in all RFID implementations.

3

COMPONENTS OF RFID SYSTEMS

Five Questions This Chapter Will Answer

- How does RFID work?
- What are the different types of RFID tags?
- What determines the size of an RFID tag?
- Why do I need to consider different operating frequencies?
- What is the purpose of the RFID middleware?

This chapter establishes the foundation required to successfully plan for RFID solutions. Here, we will provide a high-level, functional description of the most common components used in implementing RFID-based applications. We describe the RFID system components needed for solutions ranging from simple to sophisticated, and examine their functions, advantages, and limitations. Even though not every layer of technical detail is required to understand how an RFID system can be designed, it is useful to know how the various parts interoperate to form an application solution.

Because of the wide-scale interest in the adoption of RFID in supply chain applications, we also discuss the key components specified by the EPCglobal standards organization.

Specifically, this chapter will provide the following:

- An overview of basic concepts of radio frequency (RF) and the underlying physical principles behind the technology

- A description of the communication and data exchange methods between the hardware and software components of RFID systems, including the interactions with existing and new applications

- A high-level, functional description of the EPCglobal Network, a collection of components that enable creation of RFID systems compliant with the EPCglobal standards.

Operational Description of RFID Systems

In a nutshell, RFID involves detecting and identifying a *tagged* object through the data it transmits. This requires a *tag* (a.k.a. transponder), a *reader* (a.k.a. interrogator) and *antennae* (a.k.a. coupling devices) located at each end of the system. The reader is typically connected to a *host computer* or other device that has the necessary intelligence to further process the tag data and take action. The host computer is often a part of a larger network of computers in a business enterprise and, in some cases, is connected to the Internet.

This basic unit of architecture can be applied to the full spectrum of RFID-enabled solutions, whether simple or complex. For example, in a clothing store where items have an RFID tag affixed, the detection of the tag by the reader simply sets off an alarm. At the other end of the complexity spectrum is a sophisticated supply chain application where detection of a pallet of cereal boxes coming into the loading dock at a supermarket updates the inventory and triggers several other actions. It generates an update to the financial system for possible bill payment, a notification to the warehouse personnel to restock shelves, and an update to the manufacturer that the shipment has been received, possibly through an Internet or Electronic Data Interchange (EDI) connection.

One key element of operation in RFID is data transfer. It occurs with the connection between a tag and a reader, also known as *coupling*, through the antennae on either end, as shown in Figure 3.1.

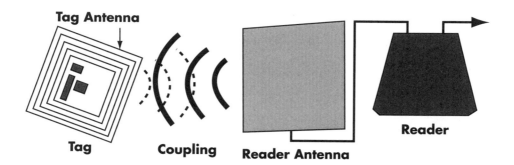

FIGURE 3.1 Connection Between Tag, Reader, and Antenna

The coupling in most RFID systems is either electromagnetic (*backscatter*) or magnetic (*inductive*). The method used in a particular implementation depends on the application requirements, such as the cost, size, speed, and read range and accuracy. For example, inductively coupled RFID systems typically have a short range, measured in inches. These types of systems are used mostly in applications, such as access control, where short range is advantageous. In this case a tag only unlocks an RFID-enabled door lock when it is moved within close range of the reader, not when people who may be carrying a tag in their wallet or purse are walking past the reader in a hallway in front of the door.

The element that enables the tag and reader communication is the antenna. The tag and the reader each has its own antenna.

Another important element in an RFID system is the frequency of operation between the tag and the reader. Specific frequency selection is driven by application requirements such as speed, accuracy, and environmental conditions, with standards and regulations that govern specific applications. For example, RFID applications for animal tagging have been operating in the 135 kHz frequency band, based on long-standing regulations and accepted standards.

What is backscatter modulation?

A common way the communication between a tag and a reader happens is through a physical principle known as backscatter modulation. In this process, a reader sends a signal (energy) to a tag, and the tag responds by reflecting a part of this energy back to the reader. A charge device such as a capacitor contained in the tag makes this reflection possible. The capacitor gets charged as it stores the energy received from the reader. As the tag responds back, it uses this energy to send the signal back to the reader. The capacitor discharges in the process.

Although hardware components are responsible for identifying and capturing data, software components of an RFID application are responsible for managing and manipulating the data transmitted between the tag and the reader and between the reader and the host computer.

Figure 3.2 shows the various RFID System components and their operational relationship with one another.

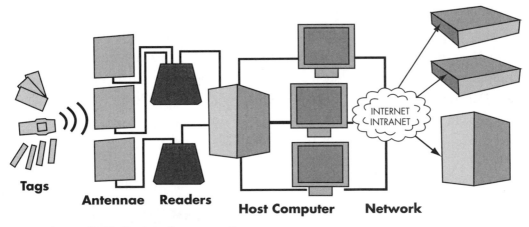

Tags   **Antennae   Readers**   **Host Computer**   **Network**

FIGURE 3.2   RFID System Components

Hardware Components

In the following sections, we describe the three common hardware components present in all RFID systems, tag, reader, and, antennae.

Tag

The tag, also known as the transponder (derived from the terms *trans*mitter and *res*ponder), holds the data that is transmitted to the reader when the tag is interrogated by the reader. The most common tags today consist of an Integrated Circuit (IC) with memory, essentially a microprocessor chip (see Figure 3.3). Other tags are *chipless* and have no onboard IC. Chipless tags are most effective in applications where simpler range of functions is all that is required; although they can help achieve more accuracy and better detection range, at potentially lower cost than their IC-based counterparts. From here on out, we will use the term *tag* to mean IC-based tag. We will refer to chipless tags explicitly, when needed.

When a tag is interrogated, the data from its memory is retrieved and transmitted. A tag can perform basic tasks (read/write from/to memory) or manipulate the data in its memory in other ways. A tag's memory attribute can be read-only (RO), write once-read many (WORM), or read-write (RW). Memory write capability generally increases the cost of a tag, along with its capability to perform higher-level functions. At the same time, read-only tags eliminate the risk of accidental or malicious over-writing of tag data.

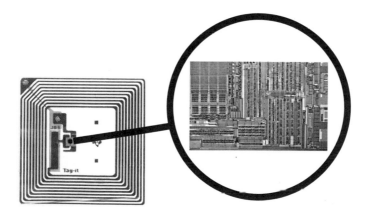

FIGURE 3.3   **A Typical Passive Tag (Left) and a Photo of a Partial Tag Microchip Design (Right)[1] (Photos Courtesy of Texas Instruments Incorporated (Left) and Celis Semiconductor Corporation (Right))**

Tag Types

The most popular tags today are passive tags. These tags have favorable form factors and can be produced at very low cost, partly because they require no battery power.

[1] The Microchip design is not for the passive tag shown here.

They get their power by harnessing the electromagnetic energy emitted from the reader. Many solutions are currently in place that employ passive tag technology, such as animal tracking, asset management, industrial automation, electronic article surveillance, and access control applications.

Unlike passive tags, active tags have a battery on board that powers the tag and allows for longer read ranges, better accuracy, more complex information exchange, and richer processing capabilities. Because active tags have their own power source, they can transmit data without requiring a reader to power (energize) them. Due to the battery, active tags have a finite lifetime. One of the more common uses for active tags is for tracking high-value objects over long ranges such as tagging and tracking of military supplies shipped around the world. However, active tags are also used in many other commercial applications where environmental conditions and application requirements demand more robust tag and reader communication. The case studies titled, "Operation Enduring Freedom/Operation Iraqi Freedom (OEF/OIF)" and "Woolworths, Plc." in Appendix A demonstrate how the same active tag technology, by Savi Technology, is being used in a military and (separately) in a commercial application to operate in very challenging environmental conditions.

There is also a class of tags called semi-active or semi-passive (the naming convention varies, depending on the tag manufacturer). This type of tag draws power from the onboard battery to "energize" and operate the tag's IC and perform simple tasks. However, it still utilizes the reader's electromagnetic field to "wake up" and draw power for transmitting the data stored in the tag back to the reader. A very common example of this tag type is electronic toll collection, in use since the 80s. Batteries used in these types of tags typically last several years because power is only consumed when the tag is activated and is in the reader's field.

Tag Packaging

Tag packaging plays an important role in the "art" of creating RFID applications. Because a tag might require embedding in or attachment to an object that varies in size, contour, and surface material, the package that delivers a tag defines, to a large degree, its usefulness.

Tag package dimensions are often defined by the size and shape of the tag's antenna. Current technology has enabled the production of flexible tags, also referred to as *smart labels*. A smart label functions like a typical adhesive label and often carries traditional printed barcode information in addition to an embedded RFID tag.

Smart labels are affixed to objects in applications such as baggage handling or asset tracking. There are even flexible tags that have an onboard battery. These tags are called smart active labels (SAL). We discuss SAL technology in more detail in Chapter 11, "Emerging Trends in RFID."

Tags can be embedded into a variety of other objects, including the following:

- Plastic cards for automatic payment

- Car keys or key chains for access control

- Glass casings for injecting under human and animal skin

- Non-digestible housings for ingesting into animal stomach

- Sew-on tags for attaching to clothing labels

- Custom hardened packaging—for example in a bolt—for industrial applications

Tag Memory Size

Tag memory is a very important element of IC-based RFID systems. Proper planning and use of tag memory can greatly enhance the functionality of an application. In certain supply chain applications, such as livestock tracking, the tag memory can be used initially to store a unique identifier. Then, at any stage in the supply chain, critical information can be updated, stored, and read. In this application, information might include health history, number of calves produced, date and location of ownership transfer, weight at the time of a sale, and so on.

Tag memory configurations can vary greatly based on cost and physical requirements. In the case of EAS (electronic article surveillance), tags have essentially 1 bit of memory and are relatively inexpensive when compared to tags with more memory. These tags have no unique identifiers and are used only to signal their presence when they are in the field of a reader. Beyond the 1-bit tags, typical memory footprints can range from 16 bits to several hundred kbits for certain active tags. The amount of memory present on a tag is then defined by application requirements and/or any relevant standards or regulations. For example, due to the expected global acceptance of the EPCglobal standards, the memory size for the newer generation of passive tags will be 2 kbits or more.

Table 3.1 shows a summary of selected tag attributes and compares their common characteristics.

TABLE 3.1   Tag Attributes and Characteristics

Attribute	Characteristics
Design	• IC-Based—Most common tag. Has integrated circuit with memory to perform simple computations. • Chipless—Relies on material properties of tag for data transmission. Can achieve higher range and better accuracy. Does not have computational power or ability to store new/additional data.
Type	• Passive—Requires no battery to operate. Offers lowest range and accuracy. Least costly. • Active—Requires battery to operate IC and to communicate with the reader. Offers highest range and accuracy. Costliest. • Semi-Active—Requires battery only to operate IC. Offers better range and accuracy than passive tags at lower cost than active tags.
Memory	• Read Only—Data written at tag manufacture time only makes tag tamper proof (native characteristic of chipless tags). • Write Once/Read Many—Ability to write data one time only makes the tag tamper resistant but provides flexibility to write data after tag manufacture time, which can significantly reduce production costs. • Read/Write—Most flexible. Vulnerable to data tampering and overwrite.

Chipless Tags

Chipless identification technology, an emerging form of RFID, has the potential to help proliferate the use of RFID technology into an even greater number of applications. Essentially passive, chipless tags lack some of the memory capabilities of their IC-based (that is, microchip) counterparts. However, they can enhance the performance of applications in other ways. In simple terms, most of the chipless technologies employ the idea of "encoding" unique patterns on the surface of various reflective materials. These patterns then become the data that will be reflected back to custom designed readers via radio waves. Chipless tags require power only to transmit radio waves. They have no chip that would require additional power as is needed for IC-based tags. Although the underlying technology in chipless tags is well beyond the scope of this book, it is important to note the following significant advantages they can offer:

- Better accuracy when reading tags around liquid or metal

- More effective handling of RF interference

- Longer read ranges

- Operation at extreme temperatures

- Capability to be embedded invisibly in paper documents

- Lower price-per-tag

Note that these features are not the attributes of all chipless technologies, but they represent the range of features that exists amongst various types of chipless technologies.

Chipless tags have been introduced into product labels, documents, and packaging. Developers of chipless tags market their technologies to medical, pharmaceutical, and consumer-packaging companies, as well as to agencies and entities concerned with intellectual property, classified information, securities, and banknotes.

Sensory Tags

Sensory tags offer the capability to monitor, measure, and record various environmental conditions. The concept is quite simple. A sensing device is packaged together with a tag to interact and record whatever condition the sensor is designed to monitor. The technology involved can get challenging if an application calls for passive sensory tags. This means first that the sensor has no power while the tag is not in a reader's range and second that the power is very limited even when there is a reader in range. Some of the more interesting sensory tags that exist today, or are under development, include tags that can detect, record, and transmit changes in air pressure, temperature, volume of liquid, or the presence of chemical or bacterial agents. There are also tamper detection tags that can be applied to products at manufacture time.

Reader

The reader, also referred to as the interrogator, is a device that captures and processes tag data (see Figure 3.4). Although some readers can also write data onto a tag, the device is still referred to as a reader or interrogator. The reader is also responsible for interfacing with a host computer. We discuss typical functions of RFID readers in the following sections.

FIGURE 3.4   Two Typical Passive RFID Readers (Photos Courtesy of Alien Technology Corporation [left] and Texas Instruments Incorporated [right])

Energize the Tag

In the case of passive and semi-active tags, the reader provides the energy required to activate or energize the tag in the reader's electromagnetic field. The reach of this field is generally determined by the size of the antenna on both sides and the power of the reader. The size of the antenna is generally defined by application requirements. However, the power of the reader (through the antenna), which defines the intensity and reach of the electromagnetic field produced, is generally limited by regulations. Each country has its own set of standards and regulations relating to the amount of power generated at various frequencies. For this reason, incompatibilities do exist between RFID systems in various countries. In Chapter 4, "Standards Related to RFID," we discuss standards and their impact on the implementation of RFID-based applications, in detail.

Define Operating Frequency

One of the more important aspects of a tag and reader connection (coupling) is the frequency at which it operates. Frequency of operation can vary based on the application, standards, and regulations. The most common RFID frequency ranges are Low Frequency (LF) at 135kHz or less, High Frequency (HF) at 13.56MHz, Ultra High Frequency (UHF) starting at 433MHz, and Microwave Frequency at 2.45GHz and 5.8GHz. In general, the frequency defines the data transfer rate (speed) between the tag and the reader. The lower the frequency, the slower the transfer rate. However, speed is not the only consideration in designing an RFID solution. Environmental conditions can play a significant role in determining the optimal operating frequency for a particular application. For example, the substrate that tags are attached to (such as cans of soda) and the presence of other radio wave producing devices (such as microwave ovens or cordless telephones) can create interference in the UHF and microwave bands respectively.

Higher frequency usually means smaller antennae, smaller tag size, and greater range—and typically, more regulatory use restrictions and often, higher cost. Table 3.2 summarizes the most popular frequency bands, and their typical uses and characteristics.

Read Data from the Tag

The most common task a reader will perform is, unsurprisingly, to read data stored on the tag. This process requires a sophisticated software algorithm to ensure reliability, security, and speed. We discuss the software required to achieve these objectives later in this chapter.

Write Data onto the Tag

For write-capable RFID systems, a reader can perform a dual function by also writing data onto a tag. This can be very useful because of the following:

- Tags can be mass-produced with no data in their memory. A reader can then be used to initialize a tag's memory based on application requirements. For example, a unique identification number can be encoded on the tag by the manufacturer of a given product immediately before the tag is applied to the product packaging.

- With a read/write tag, the data can be changed, added to or even eliminated at any point during its lifecycle.

Communicate with the Host Computer

The reader is also responsible for the flow of data between the tags and the host computer. Typically the reader communicates with a host computer through a Serial or Ethernet connection. A reader may also be equipped to communicate with the host computer through a wireless connection, particularly if the reader is a portable or handheld device. We discuss the details of the software interface between the reader and the host computer later in this chapter.

TABLE 3.2   Summary of Characteristics and Applications of Most Popular RFID Frequency Ranges

Frequency	Key Characteristics	Typical Applications
Low Frequency (LF) Less than 135KHz	• In use since 1980s and widely deployed • Works best around metal and liquid • Lowest data transfer rate • Read range measured in inches	• Animal identification • Industrial automation • Access control
High Frequency (HF) 13.56 MHz	• In use since mid 1990s and widely deployed • Common worldwide standards • Longer read range than LF tags (3+ feet) • Lower tag costs than LF tags • Poor performance around metal	• Payment and loyalty cards (Smart Cards) • Access Control • Anti-counterfeiting • Various item level tracking applications such as for books, luggage, garments, etc. • Smart shelf • People identification and monitoring
Ultra High Frequency (UHF) 433 MHz and 860 to 930 MHz	• In use since late 1990s • Longer read range than HF tags (10+ feet) • Very long transmit ranges for active 433 MHz systems (up to several hundred feet) • Gaining momentum due to worldwide retail supply chain mandates • Potential to offer lowest cost tags • Incompatibility issues related to regional regulations • Susceptible to interference from liquid and metal	• Supply chain and logistics such as: - inventory control - warehouse management - asset tracking
Microwave 2.45 GHz and 5.8 GHz	• In use for several decades • Fast data transfer rates • Common in active and semi-active modes • Read range is similar to UHF • Poor performance around liquid and metal	• Access Control • Electronic Toll Collection • Industrial Automation

What is smart labeling?

Smart labeling is a popular term often used in the consumer packaged goods industry. It refers to the application of smart labels to cases and pallets shipped from consumer packaged goods (CPG) manufacturers such as Gillette or Procter & Gamble to retailers such as Wal-Mart or Metro Group. The process involves simultaneously printing barcode information and encoding the RFID tag on a smart label to uniquely identify cases and pallets. This can be achieved by sophisticated printer/reader devices—commonly called printer/encoders—that can often apply the smart labels automatically as cases of packaged goods roll on the conveyor or get palletized.

Antenna

The antennae are the conduits for data communication between the tag and the reader. Antenna design and placement plays a significant factor in determining the coverage zone, range and accuracy of communication. For example, a so-called *linear reader antenna* offers a higher range than a *circular reader antenna*. At the same time a linear antenna will yield less accurate read results in applications where the orientation of a tag's antenna, with respect to the reader's antenna, can vary randomly. This makes the linear antenna more suitable for applications where a tagged item's orientation is always the same, such as on an automated assembly line.

The tag antenna is usually mounted on the same surface as the IC and packaged as a single unit. Figure 3.5 shows several common passive tag and antenna configurations. Although the tag IC can be tiny (the size of a grain of rice or smaller), the size and shape of the antenna typically determines the limits of the dimensions of the entire tag packaging.

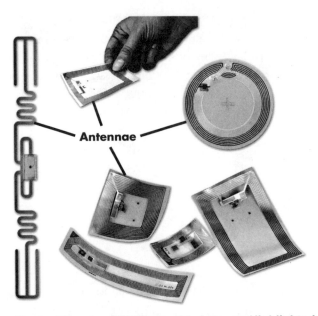

FIGURE 3.5   Some Typical Passive RFID Tags with Antenna Highlighted (Photos Courtesy of Texas Instruments Incorporated and Alien Technology Corporation—far left tag)

The packaging characteristics for the antenna on a reader also vary greatly depending on application requirements. In certain cases such as handheld readers, the antenna is mounted directly on the reader. In other cases, several antennae can be mounted away from a reader unit and positioned strategically to enhance the quality and range of the radio signals. For example, in a pallet tracking application, the reader may be connected through a network of antennae forming a well-defined detection zone such as a portal or a gate for accurate and reliable performance at the loading dock (see Figure 3.6).

FIGURE 3.6   RFID Reader and Antennae Portal (Photo Courtesy of Symbol Technologies, Inc.)

Limitations of Tag and Reader Communications

Because the science of radio frequency is analog, not digital, it is susceptible to degradation caused by interference from spurious RF noise sources and environmental conditions. Interference can be caused by proximity to the following:

- Liquid, such as water

- Metal, foil, or other metallic objects

- High humidity

- Extreme temperatures—very hot or very cold

- Motors or engines

- Wireless devices, such as cell phones and PDAs

- Wireless computer or communication networks

- Cordless phones

The degree to which these conditions affect a given RFID system's performance depends on the operating frequency. The capability to address interference issues plays a significant role in the success of an RFID deployment. For this reason, extensive trials and pilots to enable optimal placement and installation of the individual RFID components are critically important.

RF engineers are making great progress in designing systems that continue to push the RF physics to overcome some of these limitations. At the same time, many of the inaccuracies and inconsistencies also can be addressed with sophisticated software solutions that implement error correction, fault tolerance, and redundancy.

Host Computer

The hardware characteristics of a host computer are generally dependent on the type of software applications running on the computer. We therefore describe the function of the host computer in terms of the host application. The host application, described in the next section, is the collection of existing and new software programs that leverage the data generated by an RFID system. Going forward, we will use the terms *host computer* and *host application* interchangeably.

Software Components

The specific features and functionalities of the software components of an RFID system vary greatly depending on the application and requirements. These components fall into the following categories:

- RFID system software

- RFID middleware

- Host application

Software programs are executed in the tag, the reader, and the host computer.

Although we will describe each of these components separately, it is reasonable to expect cooperation and overlap of functionality between these three software components. Figure 3.7 illustrates these interdependencies and the functionality overlap between the software components.

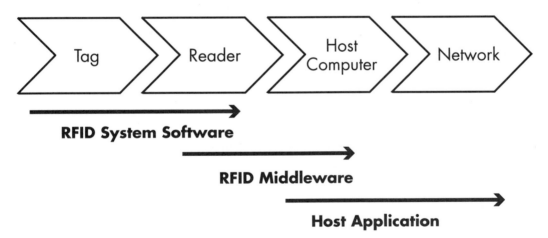

FIGURE 3.7   RFID Software Components and Their Interdependencies

RFID System Software

The RFID system software is the collection of functions necessary to enable the basic interaction between a tag and a reader. In its most basic form, the communication occurs at a radio signal processing level. It requires hardware, very low-level software (firmware), and higher-level system software to manage the data that flows between tag and reader. The following sections describe typical RFID system software functions required at the tag and reader level.

Read/Write

These are the most basic functions of a tag. A reader asks a tag to read or write data. The tag accesses its memory to read the data as instructed by the reader and transmits the data back to the reader. The tag also can be supplied data by the reader (from the host application) to write to its memory, provided the tag has write capability.

Anti-Collision

Anti-collision software is used when, at any given point in time, multiple tags are present in a reader's RF field and must be identified and tracked simultaneously. This is typical in most supply chain management applications. For example, in an inventory management application deployed in a warehouse, hundreds or even thousands of tagged objects may be within a single reader's RF field, which can be up to several feet in radius. A single pallet of RFID tagged apparel can have more than 100 cases, each containing dozens of clothing items. The anti-collision function requires cooperation between the tags and readers to minimize the risk of many tags responding all at one time. In some cases, the algorithm may be as simple as each tag waiting a random amount of time before responding to a reader's request.

Error Detection/Correction

A reader may employ sophisticated software to detect and correct transmission errors from the tag. Such software may also include programming to detect and discard duplicate or incomplete data.

Encryption, Authorization, and Authentication (Security)

Encryption, authorization, and authentication are useful when secure data exchange must occur between a tag and a reader. Both the tag and the reader must cooperate to execute the protocol needed to achieve the desired level of data security. For example, to prevent an unauthorized reader from retrieving data from a tag, the tag and the reader may have to execute an authorization protocol by exchanging a common secret or code. After this shared information has been exchanged and validated, the tag then transmits the data to the reader.

Security functionality on the tag requires sophisticated IC design and capability, which can significantly impact the cost of a typical passive tag. The topic of security is discussed in detail in Chapter 10, "Security and Privacy."

RFID Middleware

RFID middleware[2] consists of a set of software components that acts as a bridge between the RFID system components (that is, tags and readers) and the host application software. It performs two primary functions:

- Monitors device (that is, reader) health and status

- Manages RFID-specific (that is, tag and reader) infrastructure and data flow

These functions are related and often share or leverage common data. However, they fulfill very distinct application requirements and have unique characteristics. We describe each separately in the following sections. Note that most RFID middleware vendors offer software that aggregates both functions into a single package. However, as with any multifunction software package, each vendor addresses these functions with varying degrees of sophistication. Your choice of a particular vendor solution should be based on your own application requirements. We offer extensive advice in Chapter 8, "Vendor Considerations and Landscape," to help you with this choice.

Monitor

This function consists of centrally monitoring and reporting readers' health and status within an RFID-enabled application. This is an especially important function in environments where multiple readers are distributed across a single or multiple locations, and visual or manual monitoring is not practical. For example, consider a large warehouse location where multiple conveyor belts are outfitted with dozens of strategically located readers that automatically collect data on tagged items. In this case, it is important to be alerted to reader breakdowns or malfunctions as quickly as possible. This helps address the problem in real-time and reverses any error that may have occurred, in a timely fashion.

---

[2] The term middleware here should not be confused with the term middleware used in enterprise IT applications. In enterprise IT applications, middleware software is used to connect disparate pieces of enterprise application software.

In an ideal situation, the monitoring software should be able to handle devices other than readers (for example, where barcode readers or RFID smart label printer/encoders are also used).

Manage

In a nutshell, this function consists of encoding, collection, processing, filtering, and aggregation of data transmitted between tags and readers for integration with the host application. This is an especially significant function in an environment where readers can pick up large bursts or constant streams of tag data (such as in a supply chain application). Tag data needs to be cleansed—for example, to remove duplicates—massaged, or filtered, and alerts may need to be raised based on certain predefined rules for data collection.

Another important function performed at this stage is data normalization. In the absence of standards, reader data formats and communication protocols with a host are usually proprietary. To function in a multi-vendor environment, the RFID middleware software is responsible for translating various reader data formats into a single, normalized format for easier integration at the host application level.

Host Application

The host application receives processed and normalized data sent from the tag, via the reader and the RFID middleware software. The host application typically is a previously existing software program in an enterprise, such as an inventory control or warehouse management system. Depending on the sophistication of the RFID middleware and the capabilities of the host application, the host application software may not even need to know the actual source of the data it expects to receive. For example, an inventory management application can successfully track all the products on the shelves in a retail store without "knowing" how the data is entered. Before the RFID system was installed, this data may have been entered manually or through a barcode system. As long as the application has a well-defined interface protocol for data input, the RFID middleware software need only process and format the data originating from the tag and use the protocol defined by the host application to pass on this data.

However, some applications may need to be modified to accept a new set of data from the RFID middleware because they lack a fully defined interface protocol. This scenario is more likely if the application is older or home-grown.

In other situations, a different software program must be written or purchased as the host application because an entirely new solution has been deployed within the enterprise. For example, consider an RFID-based access control system implemented in a business where access control was previously achieved through metallic keys. In this case, entirely new application software is required to manage, authenticate, and provide user access.

It is important to note that a significant challenge exists, regardless of whether an existing application can handle RFID data or a new application or interface has to be developed. In many cases, RFID represents new data for an enterprise. It is unlikely that the enterprise has an existing business model that can fully leverage this data. For example, in a typical RFID-enabled supply chain management solution, items are identified by an Electronic Product Code (EPC). EPC is an extended form of UPC (Universal Product Code) used in barcode systems, and allows for encoding of much more detailed item data than UPC. Existing supply chain business models and applications originally developed to use the UPC data now have access to new, extended EPC data that they can and should leverage. This is what we referred to as the unique identification or serialization challenge in Chapter 1's "Supply Chain Integration" section. Businesses will indeed have to re-architect their business models and applications to be able to fully realize the benefits of this additional data generated through RFID systems.

The EPCglobal Network

The need for interoperability is very clear in end-to-end supply chain applications where goods move through dozens of different trading partners and businesses, each with potentially unique implementations of RFID infrastructure and application requirements. Thus, the need to have a common means of data formatting, processing, and exchange that helps these unique systems to interoperate becomes obvious. A standards organization called EPCglobal helps address this need through creation of EPCglobal standards. In the following sections, we describe the key components that enable the creation of RFID systems that are EPCglobal standards-compliant. The components are collectively referred to as the EPCglobal Network. In Chapter 4, we discuss key EPCglobal and other standards that have been ratified or are under consideration. Because EPCglobal standards are evolving rapidly, we recommend that you consult the EPCglobal Web site (*www.epcglobalinc.org*) to obtain information on the latest advancements and developments related to these standards or ask your vendors for the latest update.

Electronic Product Code (EPC)

EPC is a numbering scheme that allows assignment of a unique identifier to any physical object. It can be regarded as the next generation Universal Product Code (UPC), which is used on most products today. EPC enables the means to assign a unique identifier to each item, thus allowing every item to be uniquely identified. The current format of EPC type I data that allows this unique identification includes the following fields (see Figure 3.8):

- Header: Identifies the EPC's version number

- Manager number: Identifies the enterprise using the EPC number

- Object class: Refers to the class or category of a product, similar to a Stock Keeping Unit (SKU)

- Serial number: Identifies a unique instance of the item being tagged

This 96-bit EPC specification[3] provides unique identifiers for 268 million companies. Each company can have 16 million object classes, with 68 billion serial numbers in each class.

01 • 0000A89 • 00016F • 000169DC0
Header   EPC Manager   Object Class   Serial Number

FIGURE 3.8   EPC Numbering Format

The ID System

The ID system refers to the tag and reader components. EPC codes are stored on EPC tags that are read by EPC readers. This is the area where significant EPCglobal standards activities are focused today. Currently, several standards describe tag

---

[3] EPCglobal has also specified a 64-bit EPC format.

formats, functionality, and tag-reader communication for different types of tags (see Chapter 4 for details). The ultimate goal is to drive standards that provide common means for tags and readers from all compliant vendors to function similarly and communicate seamlessly.

EPC Middleware

In a supply chain environment where readers are picking up a nearly constant stream of EPCs, managing the data is a significant task. The EPC Middleware (sometimes known by its old name, the Savant) is responsible for managing EPC data flow between readers within an enterprise and the enterprise's existing application software. Similar to what we described earlier as RFID middleware, the EPC Middleware functions consist of collection, processing, filtering, and aggregation of data.

Object Name Service (ONS)

The ONS matches the EPC of a product to information about that product. When the EPC Middleware receives EPC data, it can query an ONS server to find out where more detailed product information is stored.

This system has been modeled after the highly scalable, reliable, and high-performance Domain Name System (DNS) system used in the Internet. When using the Internet, you can provide a URL to a DNS server and expect to receive the associated IP address. Because it is anticipated that RFID will scale to identifying trillions of products from thousands of companies using public network infrastructure, DNS design concepts were used in the design of ONS.

EPC Information Services (EPCIS)

The EPCIS component specifies the services and interfaces that are necessary to facilitate data exchange among trading partners' applications across an entire supply chain. A key feature consists of a central repository of EPC data that is shared and updated by supply chain trading partners globally. When fully implemented and adopted, EPCIS will provide the infrastructure necessary to accelerate true end-to-end supply chain integration.[4]

---

[4] We first introduced the topic of supply chain integration in Chapter 1 and will revisit it again in Chapter 11.

For additional technical details on the EPCglobal network architecture, see Appendix B, the white paper titled "The Sun EPC Network Architecture." This paper describes a typical system architecture based on the EPCglobal specifications. It demonstrates the way in which some of the key EPCglobal components come together to form the basis for building a large-scale supply chain application.

Summary

To design an RFID-enabled solution that can take full advantage of the technology, it is essential to understand both RFID system components and their functional interactions. In this chapter, we discussed the common components of all RFID systems, including both hardware (tag, reader, antennae, and host computer) and software (operating system, middleware, and host application). We also showed how these components integrate and work with each other. An overview of a standardized architecture based on these components was also provided during the discussion of the EPCglobal Network.

Successful RFID implementations also require a clear understanding of standards, people and process reengineering, cost-benefit issues, and security. You are now ready to explore these crucial topics, starting in the next chapter with a detailed discussion of standards and their role in successful RFID deployments.

PART II

HOW TO DEPLOY RFID

4

STANDARDS RELATED TO RFID

Five Questions This Chapter Will Answer

- How do standards help technology adoption?
- What are the key standards for RFID?
- What does the EPCglobal standard mean and what is EPC generation 2?
- How are standards different between the United States, Europe, and China?
- How can you ensure standards compliance in RFID deployment while the standards are evolving?

The creation and adoption of official (or *de facto*) standards can powerfully accelerate the adoption of new technology. Standards promise interoperability, luring more vendors to provide solutions that improve services and lower costs. By complying with standards, technology developers, suppliers, and vendors avoid the risk of costly modifications that may result from customized or proprietary implementations, or noncompliance with regulations. Standards give consumers the confidence that products will work together, that they will have more choices, and that they won't be subject to vendor lock-in. This has been true in one technology market after another. RFID is no exception.

In this chapter, we will do the following:

- Describe the role of standards in technology advancement

- Provide an overview of key standards around RFID and details of the EPCglobal standards

- Outline recommendations to deal with evolving standards while deploying RFID

Role of Standards in Technology Advancement and Adoption

Standards help to serve consumers in many ways. They ensure that different products don't interfere with each other's functions, regardless of which manufacturer made them. For example, a cellular phone operates at a specific frequency. These frequencies are different from the ones used to transmit television signals. As a result, a cellular phone and a television don't interfere with each other even when operating in each other's proximity.

Standards also enable interoperability between applications or devices. When a consumer buys a cellular phone complying with the GSM standard, it comes equipped with a thumbnail-sized SIMcard (Subscriber Identification Module). The card stores all the data about the phone such as the phone number and the phone book. If the consumer decides to upgrade the phone later, all he has to do is insert the old SIMcard into a new phone. His old phone number will now ring the new phone, and his phone book will be available on the new phone. The standardized SIMcard ensures seamless interoperability from one device to another.

Sometimes, a series of interdependent standards is required to help drive further advancement of a particular technology. The standards-based protocols used to transfer data on the Internet provide a good example. In this case, the standards enable a seamless transfer of data through a number of sequential interfaces. The impact of such cascading transactions that occurs from the dovetailing of standards can have a sweeping effect on entire markets, including vendors, suppliers, and consumers. Consider, for example, a business customer using a wireless laptop to enter data into an application that generates a service order. Several standards come into play in this seemingly simple scenario. Their combined effect causes a chain reaction that is powerful and dramatic in its reach, as in the following:

- A standard such as Java or XML enables successful data transfer between different applications

- Wi-Fi[1] standards enable wireless communication between the laptop and the network

- FCC standards for laptop electronic signals ensure that the user's experience is a safe one and that the signals do not interfere with other nearby devices

Working together, these standards deliver even more value than they would individually. Had these standards not been defined clearly, business users probably would have had to pay more, receive a less satisfactory result, and possibly might have failed to complete their expected transaction. When such end-to-end standards do not exist, as was the case for RFID until very recently, the technology might only be suitable for certain niche markets. With the creation of EPCglobal, though, the end-to-end RFID standards have become possible.

Standards and RFID—An Overview of EPCglobal

Prior to the development of standards for tags and readers, companies primarily developed proprietary RFID systems so that readers from one vendor often only read tags from the same vendor. Early RFID applications, such as those for electronic toll

---

[1] Wireless Fidelity, commonly known as Wi-Fi, refers to a set of standards that allow various devices such as a laptop or a Personal Digital Assistant (PDA) to connect to the network (e.g. the Internet) wirelessly. These standards are also known as IEEE 802.11x standards and exhibit data transfer throughput comparable to broadband connections.

collection, railroad asset tracking, and livestock tracking, were based on such proprietary systems. Although RFID systems can be built to operate primarily in four frequency bands (135kHz, 13.56MHz, 900MHz, or 2.45GHz), only 13.56MHz enjoys worldwide acceptance as an ISO standard (see the section, "ISO and RFID Standards," in this chapter). This lack of interoperability limited incentives for companies to implement RFID solutions broadly, and for developers to create innovative RFID technology.

This situation started changing in the late 1990s with the creation of the Auto-ID Center, headquartered at the Massachusetts Institute of Technology (MIT). It initiated the creation of a standard to facilitate full-scale interoperability between multivendor RFID systems and to propel RFID technology into a broad array of markets, notably supply chain. In 2003, the work that started under the auspices of the Auto-ID Center developed into a separate non-profit organization, EPCglobal. A joint venture between the European Article Numbering (EAN) Council and the Uniform Code Council (UCC), EPCglobal established and supports the Electronic Product Code (EPC) as the worldwide standard for immediate, automatic, and accurate identification of any item in the supply chain. EPCglobal is sponsored by many of the world's leading corporations. It has published a set of protocol standards known as Version 1.0 specifications[2]. The university lab of the former Auto-ID Center still exists at MIT, and is now referred to as Auto-ID Labs. It continues to do research on Auto-ID (RFID) related topics.

Version 1.0/1.1 Specifications

EPCglobal's Version 1.0 specifications define the overall system and various functional requirements, such as specific encoding schemes, and communications interfaces for RFID systems using class 0 (read-only) or class 1 (read/write) tags. These specifications enable standards-based communication between tags and readers to enable interoperability. Key points are described here:

- **Electronic Product Code (EPC) Tag Data Specification Version 1.1:** A supplier can use these specifications to map various identification schemes (many of them used globally) into an Electronic Product Code (EPC) code that

---

[2] Since the organization is called EPCglobal, the standards and specifications developed by it should technically be called EPCglobal standards. However, they are commonly referred to as EPC standards. We use both terms interchangeably in this book.

uniquely identifies each item. As explained in Chapter 3, "Components of RFID Systems," an RFID system identifies and tracks an item based on its EPC. The back-end software uses these specifications to associate the item and the corresponding data to other identification schemes used by many existing applications. These identification schemes include the following:

- EAN.UCC Global Trade Item Number (GTIN)

- EAN.UCC Serial Shipping Container Code (SSCC)

- EAN.UCC Global Location Number (GLN)

- EAN.UCC Global Returnable Asset Identifier (GRAI)

- EAN.UCC Global Individual Asset Identifier (GIAI)

- A General Identifier (GID)[3]

One of the key benefits of this specification is the capability to uniquely identify and track each object (also known as serialization). Without this, item level tracking and anti-counterfeit measures would not be possible. Several other issues can also arise without these specifications. For example, the tag data wouldn't be understood or acted upon by other applications, diminishing its usefulness, or the existing applications would have to be rewritten to read the tag data, requiring a significant expenditure for companies.

- **900MHz Class 0 Radio Frequency (RF) Identification Tag Specification:** Specifies the interface and the protocol (air interface and command set) for enabling communications between a tag and a reader for a 900MHz (UHF) Class 0 operation, including RF and tag requirements, and operational algorithms. Class 0 tags are read-only tags that are programmed with an EPC at manufacture time in the factory. The specifications also define 64- and 96-bit tag structures and functionalities required of the tag. Developers can use the test specifications provided to make sure that the tags comply with the specifications. Supply chain is the primary application of the tags conforming to these standards. The so-called Class 0+ tags provide both read and write capabilities.

---

[3] Details of various existing numbering schemes such as GTIN, SSCC, and GID are not discussed here as these schemes are not created for RFID. Interested readers should refer to appropriate organizations' Web sites for details.

- **13.56MHz ISM Band Class 1 Radio Frequency (RF) Identification Tag Specification:** Specifies the interface and the protocol for enabling communications between a tag and the reader for a 13.56MHz (HF) Class 1 operation, including RF and tag requirements. Class 1 tags can be WORM (Write Once, Read Many) or Read/Write tags, that is, they allow writing of new information on the tag any time during their lives through an authorized reader. Such tags are quite useful for keeping item-related dynamic data, such as pedigree and modifications to the item due to assembly, on the tag. Because ISO standards on RFID also use this frequency band, you are likely to find many RFID applications in this frequency range today. This specification may provide a path to ensure interoperability among some of the infrastructure required for such applications.

- **860MHz–930MHz Class 1 Radio Frequency (RF) Identification Tag Specification:** Specifies the interface and protocol for enabling communications between a tag and the reader for a class 1 operation (that is, WORM or Read/Write), including RF and tag requirements. This frequency falls in the UHF range.

Another EPC tag to reader interface standard that holds great promise for hardware interoperability is EPC UHF Generation 2 standard, commonly known as the gen 2 standard. Tags complying with this standard feature Read/Write capabilities (that is, Read and Write many times) and can communicate equally well with readers operating at various frequencies between 860 MHz and 930 MHz. This range includes UHF reader frequencies used in both North America and Europe. For global companies, the benefits are obvious. The goods tagged with gen 2 tags can be shipped globally, and be read by the local UHF reader infrastructure, eliminating the need for applying different types of tags on goods based on their destination. The gen 2 standard was ratified in December 2004, and will likely be aligned with ISO 18000–6 standards in the near future.

In addition, EPCglobal facilitates development of various other protocols and specifications, as follows:

- *Reader Protocol* defines the communications (messaging and protocol) between tag readers and EPC middleware.

- *Middleware Specification* (transformed from the old *Savant Specification*) defines the middleware services such as tag data collection, filtering, and reader management.

- *Physical Markup Language (PML) Core Specification, and Extensible Markup Language (XML) Schema and Instance Files* establish a vocabulary set to be used as a reference for communication between applications.

- *Object Name Service (ONS) Specification* specifies how the ONS is used to locate meta-data and services associated with an EPC.

These specifications provide the backbone for creating an EPC-compliant RFID implementation. Table 4.1 provides a summary of various EPC specifications, their status, and what parts of the RFID system they refer to.

TABLE 4.1 Summary of Various EPCglobal Standards

Standard	Status	Key Characteristics
EPC Tag Data Specification Version 1.1	• Ratified March 2004	• Allows companies to create a unique Electronic Product Code (EPC) for each item, enabling item serialization
900 MHz Class 0 Tag Specification (UHF) 13.56 MHz Class 1 Tag Specification (HF) 860–930 MHz Class 1 Tag Specification (UHF) *Class 1 = Read/Write tag* *Note: Class 0 = Read-only tag,*	• Ratified November 2004	• Specifies air interface and protocols for communication between tags and readers at this frequency / frequency range • Tags and readers complying with a specific frequency standard can interoperate with the same from another vendor • Tags and readers generally cannot interoperate with the same from another manufacturer that operates at a slightly different frequency within the frequency range (e.g. UHF range of 860–930 MHz) • So called, generation 1 tags/readers. Class 0 tags feature Read-only capability. Class 1 feature WORM (Write Once, Read Many) capability. Some may allow Read / Write many times
UHF Generation 2 Standard	• Ratified December 2004	• Tags and readers can work equally well across the spectrum of EPC UHF frequency, providing maximum interoperability compared to generation 1 tags / readers • Evolution of Class 0 and 1 UHF tag specifications • Tags feature improved Read / Write (many times) capabilities • Tags feature improved performance in dense reader environment

TABLE 4.1   continued

Standard	Status	Key Characteristics
Middleware Specification	• Application Level Events (ALE): In Development • Reader Protocol: In Development • Reader Management: In Development	• Provides middleware specifications for filtering, data collection, and reader management • Reader protocol (reader-middleware communication): upon ratification, software built on this specification will allow EPCglobal subscribers to purchase and install readers from many manufacturers and be assured they will be interchangeable. This specification will also allow reader manufacturers to build off a solid base and focus their efforts on additional functionality and lower cost. • Reader management: Software built on the Reader Management Specification will allow companies to manage arrays of readers much like they do with personal computers and printers within their existing infrastructure.
EPC Information Services (EPCIS)	• In Development	• Provides a gateway between trading partners (via the EPCglobal Network) and the RFID infrastructure of tags and readers • Defines a set of services to enable track and trace and other events based on raw tag data. Specifications useful in leveraging RFID data in decision support systems

EPCglobal continues to work on developing new standards and refining the existing ones in successive versions. Standards for semi-active (or semi-passive) and active tags are expected in future. For more details, see Standards Development Process Specification at *www.epcglobalinc.org*.

Several issues remain, though. Some of them are inherent to the standardization process, where vendors use the process to gain competitive advantage—for example, standards that result in royalties for one vendor or a small group of vendors, based on their patents. Many standardization bodies have gone around this issue by having the participating vendors donate their patents in a patent pool that is generally available to participating companies royalty-free, provided they reciprocate and use the patents to create standards-based products. However, if the resulting delay makes the standardization process too slow, some vendors may decide to bypass the standard altogether. Another issue that can hurt or slow down standardization is practicality of the implementation of a particular standard. For example, most countries have allocated 13.56MHz (HF) frequency for RFID use. However, the UHF frequency allocation is not consistent across the world. North America and Europe use 915MHz and 868MHz for UHF RFID systems (respectively), but other countries haven't followed suit. In some countries, this frequency range is already allocated for other uses, such as mobile phone or taxi communications. In these cases, government intervention will be required to sort out the resulting frequency conflict. Power generated by the antenna (reader) is another issue. European countries are stricter in terms of the amount of power an antenna is allowed to generate, compared to North America. The lower the power, the lesser the read range of the reader, affecting designs of RFID gates and other systems.

The next section describes the roles that several of the EPC elements play in the creation of an EPC compliant RFID implementation.

Implementation of EPC through EPCglobal Network

Key components that enable the creation of RFID systems compliant with EPCglobal standards are collectively referred to as the EPCglobal Network. The collection includes five key components: the Electronic Product Code (EPC) itself, the identification system (EPC-compliant tags and readers), EPC Middleware, the Object Name Service (ONS), and the EPC Information Services (EPCIS). These five components, all described in Chapter 3, "Components of RFID Systems," comprise a reference architecture that businesses worldwide can use to design their RFID deployments.

Are all five elements required for an enterprise to deploy a standards-compliant RFID solution? That depends on your requirements. As a practice, we think that the standards-based approach provides the best investment protection in the long run and should be followed. However, the whole architecture may not be needed from the start to get an RFID deployment underway in the enterprise.

For example, the first phase of an RFID deployment project may only use the EPC specifications (to tag the relevant items), the EPC compliant tags and readers (to detect and track them), the EPC Middleware (to collect the item-related information, process it, and transmit it to other decision support systems), and EPCIS.

However, ONS need not be used. In fact, Wal-Mart is using this approach (explained in more detail in Chapter 9, "Mandates as Business Catalysts"). After the RFID deployment gets integrated in the business processes, you may further enhance it by leveraging a service such as ONS.

In a slightly different scenario, you may have a business need that requires the use of both active and passive tags. The EPC specifications for active tags are not finalized, so part of your deployment may not be EPC compliant. Because you have a business need, it is prudent to proceed with proper planning that allows flexibility. For example, you may deploy such an environment after checking with your middleware vendor and verifying that it has an acceptable roadmap for supporting EPC standards as they are finalized. When the vendor supports the finalized EPC standard for active tags at a future date, your deployment may become EPC compliant with a middleware upgrade. In the following chapters, we provide a framework to enable you to look for and address such issues.

Functions and Features of EPCglobal

EPCglobal continues to work with Auto-ID Labs and the industry to facilitate the creation of EPCglobal standards and related specifications. This is achieved through ongoing communications between the researchers and end users via technical committees, action groups, and steering committees. Each group focuses on a specific area or topic, ensuring that the organization's standards creation process is primarily user-driven. The following list describes the groups as well as the structure of EPCglobal as some of you may decide to get more closely involved in the standards creation process through participation in these groups:

- Business Steering Committee (BSC) oversees the Business Action Group (BAG) and related working groups. It ensures synergy across various groups and drives proper prioritization of deliverables and resources. It also makes recommendations to the president and the board.

- Technical Steering Committee (TSC) reviews standards requests and functional requirements, and ensures that the proposed solution is consistent with EPCglobal Network architecture. It oversees and assigns technical development tasks to Technical Action Group (TAG). The committee also has representatives from the Auto-ID Labs and EAN.UCC.

- The Business Action Group (BAG) identifies industry needs, gathers requirements, develops use cases, and drives consensus on best practices. The use cases are submitted as vertical or horizontal industry-specific standards development requests. It also reviews and approves technical specifications against use cases and other business requirement documents. The BAG members are required to be EPCglobal subscribers. BAG also creates working groups focused on specific topics, as needed.

- The Technical Action Group (TAG) facilitates the development of technical standards based on business needs and requirements. A Hardware Action Group focuses on standards and specifications related to hardware issues, whereas a Software Action Group focuses on standards and specifications related to software interoperability. The action group members are required to be EPCglobal subscribers. Additionally, the Technical Action Group members are required to sign EPCglobal's Intellectual Property policy.

- Each working group, composed of a subset of action group members and EPC staff members, is responsible for completing specific tasks specified by the action groups. For example, business focused working groups create use cases, whereas technically focused workgroups create draft specifications for various standards.

- In addition, a Policy Steering Committee (PSC) works on issues that span business and technology charters, for example, privacy.

- All the steering committees, action groups, and working groups are overseen by the president of EPCglobal and a board of governors. They are responsible for setting the strategic direction of EPCglobal and ratification of the standards. The board is comprised of representatives from end-user companies and EAN organizations.

EPCglobal also offers training and education on implementing and using the EPC and EPCglobal Network to its subscribers. The organization's Web site (*www.epcglobalinc.org*) provides further contact and cost information for becoming a subscriber.

Although EPCglobal focuses on developing the comprehensive standards for interoperability among different components of an RFID implementation, various other related organizations are also focusing on standards related to RFID. It is critical that the EPC standards co-exist with them in order to ensure end-to-end interoperability of RFID systems. The world's largest developer of standards, International Organization for Standardization (ISO), has developed several standards around RFID. Because of ISO's role in the development of global standards, EPCglobal officials have decided to align their proposed standards with those of ISO. In addition, EPCglobal plans to ratify and use all applicable ISO standards. The next section provides an overview of existing ISO standards related to RFID.

ISO and RFID Standards

The International Organization for Standardization (ISO) is a network of the national standards institutes of 148 countries, based on one member per country, coordinated by its headquarters in Geneva, Switzerland. Although ISO is a non-government organization, many of its member institutes are either part of their countries' governments or mandated to develop standards by their governments, making it more global and governmental than EPCglobal. ISO bridges the needs of the public and private sectors, focusing on creating standards and building universal consensus for the acceptance of those standards. Since its inception in 1947, ISO has published more than 13,000 international standards for many different industries.

Some of these standards seem simplistic on the surface, such as ISO 8601, governing the date and time format. Yet, when you consider the worldwide worries that resulted from the so-called Y2K bug, you can understand the impact of such global standards. Among the key ISO standards that affect RFID technology are the following:

- **ISO 11784, 11785, and 14223:** These standards contain the structure of the radio frequency identification code for animals. ISO 14223 specifies the air interface between the RFID transceiver and advanced transponder used for identification of animals, based on the condition of compatibility according to ISO 11784-5.

- **ISO 10536, 14443, and 15693:** These standards cover the physical characteristics, air interface and initialization, and anti-collision and transmission protocol of vicinity cards (contactless integrated circuit cards, also known as smart identification cards). They also apply to proximity cards, covering areas such as radio frequency power and signal interface. The tags in these smart cards are capable of multiple applications so the same card can be used for building access, computer login, and cafeteria payment.

- **ISO 10374:** This standard specifies all necessary user requirements for the automatic identification of freight containers (for example, rail and ship), including a container ID system, data coding systems, description of data, performance criteria, and security features.

- **ISO 15961, 15962, and 15963:** These standards apply to automatic identification and data capture techniques for item management. Included are RFID guidelines for item management, including data protocol, application interface, data encoding rules, logical memory functions, and unique identification for RF tags.

- **ISO 18000 Series:** Several standards in the 18000 series focus on RFID for item management. ISO 18000 parts 1 through 6 address the parameters for Air Interface Communications for globally accepted frequencies such as 135kHz, 13.56MHz, UHF band, 2.45GHz, and 5.8GHz. ISO 18046 focuses on RFID tag and interrogator performance test methods, whereas 18047 covers RFID device conformance test methods. This standard is similar to the EPCglobal standard and the likely point of alignment between the two standard bodies.

Other Standardization Initiatives

In addition to ISO and EPCglobal, several other organizations have developed RFID as well as automatic data capture related standards. Although the comprehensive treatment of these is out of the scope of this book, we mention a few of them here.

A key player in the development of ISO standards has been the United States' representative, the American National Standards Institute (ANSI). ANSI is a private, non-profit organization chartered with administering and coordinating the U.S. standardization system. Particularly relevant to RFID is the standard known as ANSI 256 (INCITS 256-2001), which establishes a technical standard for a family of compatible RFID devices. It defines a common Application Programming Interface (API) between RFID tag and reader software. Eventually, this standard should provide such APIs for several different UHF and HF frequency bands. APIs for frequencies such as 2.45GHz and 433MHz have already been provided.

Another player in the RFID standards development is China. With thousands of factories in China manufacturing goods that are exported all over the globe, it is only natural that companies looking to gain total supply chain visibility start by tagging the products when they are manufactured in China. It costs more to tag these products after they arrive in the U.S. than to tag them at the time of manufacturing. In addition, the Chinese manufacturers can use RFID to gain visibility into their domestic supply chain. However, China lacks RFID standards as well as open frequencies for tag-reader communication. As a result, relatively fewer companies have deployed RFID in their Chinese operations. To remedy this situation, the Chinese government set up a working group in early 2004 to define RFID standards and protocols for the country. It is unclear how these standards will interoperate with EPCglobal and in what timeframe.

Alignment between ISO and EPCglobal standards (and even some of the country-specific ones such as the Chinese standards) would be a huge step forward for successful deployment of RFID on a global basis. It is important enough that large customers, such as the United States Department of Defense (DoD), are encouraging this movement. But what should you do in the mean time? To find out, proceed to the next section.

Recommendations for the Practitioner

- **Develop plans based on established standards, while staying alert to developments in the various standards organizations.** Although RFID standards do exist (such as the published specifications of EPCglobal, ISO, and ANSI), they are continuing to evolve. If you are a supply chain practitioner, subscribe to EPCglobal and remain alert to new developments. Make sure that you select a vendor that has a roadmap to adopt any new standards and upgrade its existing customers. Whether you are in the public or private sector, seek compliance with applicable ISO standards. If possible, participate in one of the working groups or action groups.

- **Negotiate with your technology vendor to protect yourself from legal uncertainties related to standards.** Because many technology vendors use the standards process to gain competitive advantage, lawsuits related to patent infringement are not uncommon. Although many patent holders avoid taking such lawsuits to end users (typically, they ask the vendor infringing on their patent to pay damages or royalty), you should protect yourself against this threat by negotiating a contract that the technology vendor defends you in such situations and, if necessary, fixes your deployment appropriately.

- **Create a time allowance to continually reassess how to utilize the benefits of RFID to improve your investment returns.** Stay alert to related pilots conducted by other companies in your industry or government agencies by reading trade publications and subscribing to related newsletters, as you may be able to leverage the results of such RFID technology for your own purposes. Leverage the guidelines provided by standards organizations in your decision-making. As we mentioned earlier in the mixed tag (active and passive) example, a phased approach to deployment may let you achieve compliance or gain the benefits of RFID, while keeping your options open to key developments such as the EPCIS and gen 2.

- **Make decisions based on standards, integrating relevant guidelines into your processes.** As you redesign your business processes to take advantage of RFID's benefits, make sure that the architecture is standards-based. In addition, depending on your role in the supply chain, adhere to Internet standards such as Java and XML. This will make it easier to create flexible and robust deployment architecture.

Summary

Standards play a critical role in mainstream deployment of a technology by providing interoperability of components and reducing the risk of regulatory noncompliance. They help increase the overall size of the industry by luring more suppliers (who enter the industry due to the level playing field enabled by standards) and by stimulating more consumer demand (who are more likely to deploy a standards-based technology that doesn't lock them into using one vendor's services). Early RFID deployments were based on proprietary technology used to communicate between the tag and the reader; as a result, these were confined to specific markets. With the emergence of EPCglobal, standards-based RFID deployment is becoming a reality. As with any standardization effort, co-existence of various standards (EPCglobal, ISO, and ANSI) and balancing of industry interests with broader standardization goals is going to be critical to the sustained success of the standards, and eventually the industry. You should plan to deploy standards-based RFID systems while focusing on results and Return on Investment (ROI).

The question remains, though: How do you decide whether to move forward on an RFID project? In the next several chapters, we outline a framework you can follow to decide *when* to move forward, *how* to move forward, and *what* you need to move forward.

5

FRAMEWORK FOR DEPLOYMENT

Five Questions This Chapter Will Answer

- How do I start an RFID project in a systematic way?
- What deliverables should I look for at the end of each step?
- What are the key pitfalls to avoid at each step?
- How do I scope my project and select the right pilot?
- What did other companies in my situation do to deploy RFID (that is, what are some real-life examples)?

You have seen examples of how RFID can help a business, learned about the history of RFID technology, and reviewed the components of an RFID system. You have also reviewed key RFID standards and learned how you can leverage them to build a robust RFID solution. Now it is time to answer the next question: "What steps do you take to deploy RFID in your company?"

Successful deployment of RFID technology in an enterprise requires thorough understanding of the business problem, careful planning, and optimal organizational capability to execute on the plan. An ad-hoc approach to deploying RFID is not likely to yield optimal benefits. In fact, it can distract an enterprise from its goals and harm the business. In this chapter, we will cover the following:

- Lay out a framework that shows how an enterprise decision maker can understand the problem, evaluate potential solutions from short-term and long-term risk/reward points of view, and carry out a successful implementation.

- Provide real-world examples to clarify the points.

> **Note:**
>
> Many of the examples provided in this chapter, Chapter 6, "Organizational Mobilization," and Chapter 7, "Cost-Benefit Analysis," are derived from real-life case studies based on interviews with industry practitioners like you. Details on some of these case studies are provided in Appendix A for your reference.

Introducing RFID Deployment Framework

Fundamentally, a decision to deploy RFID technology in an enterprise is a business decision, not a technology decision. It should be driven by business drivers such as increasing competitive advantage, creating new services to deliver more value to customers, streamlining operations, or complying with rules and regulations. If a decision is driven only by the "coolness" or "buzz" of the technology, it will likely not lead to maximum benefits.

How do you ensure that RFID technology is being adopted for the right reasons? Through alignment of strategy and execution. Alignment is the process of integrating business strategy with technology strategy and providing the right organizational infrastructure for execution. Such alignment ensures that the technology strategy of an organization is driven from the business strategy. Process and organization reengineering follow this step.

A conceptual framework can act as an effective guide to ensure alignment. It provides a structured way to do the following:

- Identify the problem and surrounding issues

- Define possible solutions and their attractiveness (return on investment, or ROI)

- Create a plan for successful deployment and support

In Figure 5.1, we outline a simple yet effective framework to arm you for a successful RFID deployment. Each part of the framework represents a major phase of an RFID deployment project. Each phase builds upon the previous one. Successful completion of one phase paves the way for moving the project to the next phase. We provide a set of questions that must be answered for successful completion of each phase. In addition, we list a sample set of deliverables for each phase. Several examples are illustrated to provide real-world verification of the concepts. Review of this material should help you properly plan for your RFID project and prepare in advance for possible areas of complication. Such planning should help accelerate your overall deployment timeframe. Note that these questions and deliverables are samples only. They are likely to be different from one enterprise to the next. Nonetheless, they should provide a good starting point for a practitioner to build upon.

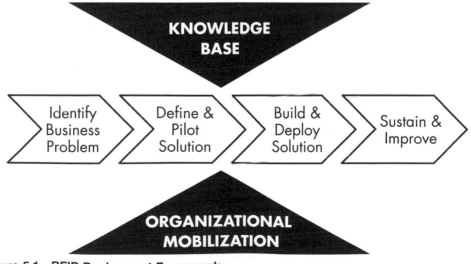

Figure 5.1 RFID Deployment Framework

The following sections look at the framework in detail. Note that the description is kept at a conceptual level and is not intended to replace a project management tool. Many project and process management tools are commercially available that can be used for that purpose. Many consulting and systems integration companies have their own proprietary tools. The selection of those tools depends on factors beyond the scope of this book. On the other hand, no matter which tool or consulting company you decide to go with, the framework that follows should provide a checklist to supplement detailed project plans produced by those tools.

Identify Business Problem

Identifying the business problem is a very critical step in IT deployment projects. Yet, many times it is overlooked or not addressed properly. A clear business rationale for deploying RFID technology should be established and agreed upon by key stakeholders in the enterprise. For example, line management, operations, and IT groups might be key stakeholders. The rationale should clearly identify what business problem the RFID deployment will solve and what the expected results are. Stakeholder buy-in is critical. Otherwise, one group's needs may be satisfied through the project, but the overall organization's needs may not. Such an exercise also sets the expectations correctly for various groups and defines the scope and boundary of the project, preventing project creep—that is, changing requirements or constant addition of new requirements that a project must meet.

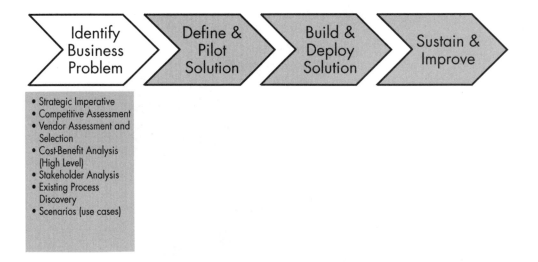

Key factors to consider in this phase are as follows:

- **Strategic Imperative:** It is it important to determine why it is critical for the organization to solve this business problem. It could be competitive pressure (as in Wal-Mart's RFID mandate forcing other retailers to follow suit); new regulations or mandates (as in the case of suppliers of Wal-Mart or the U.S. Department of Defense (DoD)); fit with strategic direction of the organization (for example, the company decides to compete based on being the cost leader, and supply chain visibility offered by RFID is seen as a key enabler for streamlining operations to minimize cost); or response to external conditions (for example, the Smart and Secure Tradelanes (SST) initiative described in Appendix A, which was partly undertaken to mitigate the security risk that a large-scale terrorist event could shut down ports and strangle trade).

- **Competitive Assessment:** It is important to understand what the competitors are doing, and how the proposed solution will affect the organization's competitive positioning. For example, if a competitor is using RFID for a very broad set of operations and if your organization is looking at a narrow application with limited benefits, which prevents your organization from leapfrogging the competition, it may be time to rethink the scope of the project.

- **Vendor Assessment and Selection:** Finding the right vendors who can address your issues is critical. The enterprise's knowledge base about the vendor landscape and track record should be heavily leveraged. (For more information, see the "Knowledge Base" section later in this chapter as well as Chapter 8, "Vendor Considerations and Landscape.") Gaps in that knowledge base should be filled with outside consultants. Many times, these consultants can act as project managers or prime contractors, and help with the execution of subsequent phases of the deployment. Several companies specialize in this area. Special attention should be given to vendors who offer better investment protection, such as open standards-based product road maps and verifiable references. Note that the choice of vendors may need to be modified based on the results of the pilot. This can add significant cost and delays to the project, so it is critical that the vendor selection is done after careful research and evaluation of criteria mentioned in Chapter 8.

- **Cost-Benefit Analysis (High Level):** A high-level cost-benefit analysis is essential for a quick go/no-go decision and determination of the project scope and resource requirements. For example, if an organization can do item-level tagging of all its goods cost effectively only if the tag price is less than 15 cents, the current tag pricing will make it ineffective to do item-level tagging. In this case, the stakeholders need to determine if the project still makes sense (go/no-go) or if they need to re-adjust the scope of the project (for example, focus only on case- and pallet-level tagging). In case of Woolworths, Plc. (see case study described in Appendix A), it was understood that the full roll-out would yield enough benefits for the project to pay for itself in one year. The current cost of tags may not be as much of an issue for a company that makes relatively high value items such as electronics or certain prescription medicines and where introduction of item level tagging may significantly reduce shrinkage or counterfeit goods. Key factors affecting cost-benefit analysis are addressed in a separate chapter.

- **Stakeholder Analysis:** A stakeholder is any person or entity that is affected by the outcome of a business process and has interest in controlling that outcome to a desired level. A business problem can touch multiple stakeholders. Some of them may not be directly related to the business process. For example, an RFID pilot (sometimes referred to as a Proof of Concept or a PoC) in a manufacturing plant involves several stakeholders. Some of the stakeholders, such as the plant operators, its IT staff, and the supervisor, can be very close to the project. However, the senior management and the finance person are also stakeholders. If the senior management of that plant or division has not bought off on the pilot, it may not allocate the right resources to the project, or may not empower the team in the right way through proper setting of goals and metrics. If the finance department has not bought off on the pilot, the requisite purchase orders for sourcing of parts may be delayed. When the right stakeholders are found, it is important to understand their motivations for (or against) the project. Some of them may have to change the way they have operated for years. For others, it may involve loss of power, resources, or title. Others may be looking at gaining more power and resources. Stakeholders may not readily convey their motivations or may convey negative motivations. For example, the fork-lift operator in the plant may be worried about the need to learn one more process or may not be completely convinced that this is a worthwhile effort. The senior management team may have wrong expectations about the delivery timeline for the results. Unless the expectations of the stakeholders are known up front and reset (in some cases), the project may not succeed fully. The next chapter describes in detail how to mobilize various stakeholders in an organization.

- **Existing Process Discovery:** If a process exists for solving the same business problem or a variant, it should be documented and its capabilities analyzed. In some cases, modifying the existing process might be more economical or less risky than starting from scratch. For example, the existing infrastructure designed to leverage data from the barcode in a manufacturing environment might be modified to take advantage of the additional data obtained from RFID tags. In other cases, the existing process might prove to be a step in a planned transition to the new process. In the preceding example, if the existing infrastructure can't handle additional data, it can be used to process the data elements from RFID tags that correspond to barcode data. The rest of the data can be processed later when the subsequent stages of the project improve the infrastructure to handle additional data from RFID tags. During the discovery, pay special attention to processes that enable data synchronization and network enablement of applications. If you don't have a proper process to share data with your customers and/or suppliers in a timely manner, the process should be corrected as part of the architecture. Likewise, if key business applications are not network enabled (that is, they operate in their own silos without proper communication interfaces to others, or require a very cumbersome communication mechanism), the architecture must specify steps to make them network enabled.

- **Scenarios:** Also known as *use cases*, these can act as very powerful planning and risk mitigation tools. This is especially useful in complex, cross-divisional, or cross-enterprise projects. RFID deployments tend to fit this description well, as they can require significant behavior and process change across an enterprise, and sometimes across companies (for example, among supply chain partners). Scenarios can also act as contingency plans. For example, a hospital might create two RFID deployment scenarios: the first for aggressive implementation across the board, based on assumptions about the technology maturing fast (cheaper and more reliable) and providing very high benefits, and the second scenario for a staged roll-out, allowing technology to mature. The second scenario can also double as a back-up scenario should budget constraints force the hospital to do staged roll-out of the technology.

Typical questions to ask in this phase include the following:

- Is the strategic rationale for embarking on this project clear?
- Are all the business stakeholders identified and onboard for further exploration?
- Do you understand enough about the technology and the process to figure out likely outcomes? Are they acceptable?
- What are the drivers of cost-benefit, and what is the most likely cost-benefit scenario?
- How will the likely outcome affect competitive position?
- Can existing business processes be modified to adopt RFID, or do new ones need to be created?
- Have alternatives been considered?

Avoid the following situations:

- Unclear rationale for starting the project or lack of understanding about how the project will improve the competitive situation
- Lack of commitment from relevant stakeholders
- Cost-benefit analysis solely based on the most optimistic projections
- Insufficient focus on technical architecture leading to data synchronization or other issues that prevent fulfillment of business needs

The output of this stage should be a project requirements document, which captures clear project requirements. It is a good idea to make sure that the key points raised in this section are addressed in this document.

Define and Pilot Solution

This phase bridges the gap between identification of a business problem and wide-scale deployment of a solution to solve that problem. This is a critical link in any enterprise-wide deployment. It provides an opportunity to test the solution in a more controlled environment while preparing detailed plans for a full-scale roll-out.

Although it may seem that focusing on the pilot first can slow down the deployment process, skipping this step can lead to costly consequences. For example, improper problem definition leading to a suboptimal solution may not be caught until the wide-scale roll-out of the solution. At that point, the company may have to engage in costly reengineering efforts. Worse, the lost time and money can adversely affect the enterprise's competitive positioning. On the other hand, a well-defined solution can be developed and deployed rapidly, leading to faster time to market.

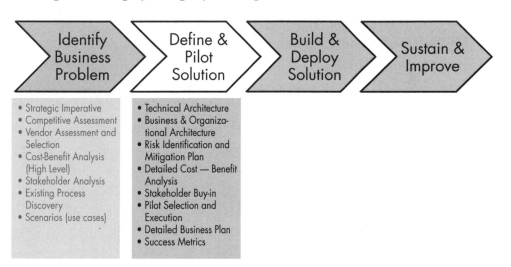

Key factors to consider in this phase are as follows:

- **Technical Architecture:** Definition of a robust and scalable technical architecture is critical in this phase. If the systems can't handle the amount of data generated through RFID tags or if there is no decision support system set up to process this data, the solution won't be as effective. The architecture should support business needs 24/7 through high availability. It should also specify the right data models (data to be captured and processed) that are flexible and expandable, so the solution can interact with various existing applications. This ensures that all applications have access to the same data (also known as data synchronization), so decisions are not made based on stale data. In the case of the Woolworths Plc. pilot, the technology and business architectures were designed to collect and integrate asset-tracking data from barcode, RFID systems, and GPS (Global Positioning System) to construct an overall asset visibility solution. After the position of a truck (carrying goods) was determined through a GPS, the distribution center (DC) was able to pinpoint the location of the goods in real-time by looking up the RFID data from the loading dock to determine which goods were in which truck. As a truck stopped at a Woolworths store and unloaded its goods, the RFID readers in the store would detect the change and update the central system in the DC. The central system would continue to track the truck, but would show an updated list of goods inside the truck. Last but not least, the architecture should adhere to industry standards to avoid vendor lock-in and ensure investment protection from changing standards or proprietary technology that becomes obsolete.

- **Business and Organizational Architecture:** If the right business and organizational architecture is not set, the project may never move past the pilot state. The goals of various stakeholders should be aligned and attached to the project. The right business processes should be set up to leverage the data collected. Rules of engagement and accountability should be clearly established to avoid confusion and drive quick decision-making. Detailed process flows should be developed here. A check should be performed to make sure that the solution still supports the strategic direction of the company. For example, when Sun Microsystems deployed an internal RFID pilot in its manufacturing plant (see Sun Microsystems case study described in Appendix A), it created a virtual team consisting of members from the manufacturing unit, Sun's professional services consultants, and engineers from the RFID product team to assemble the right skill set in one team. The team shared the same goal of rolling out the pilot and validating the cost-benefit scenario. Due to the right level of skill set and goals, the team was able to achieve its objective in the desired timeframe.

- **Risk Identification and Mitigation Plan:** Risk is inherent in any project. Even the best laid plans can go wrong. Risks can be internal to the organization or external. For example, internally, an architect may miss a delivery deadline for the architecture, delaying the testing phase and risking on-time completion. At an external level, the supplier may run into production issues, affecting the delivery time to the enterprise. Another risk is the time required to convert stand-alone business applications into network-centric applications so they can receive data from the RFID system and use it properly. A well-crafted risk identification and mitigation plan identifies potential internal and external risk factors and provides solutions to minimize or nullify their impact on the schedule. At the very least, such a plan should be developed for deliverables in the critical path of the project.

- **Cost-Benefit Analysis (Detailed):** A detailed cost-benefit analysis should be carried out in this phase to make a final go/no-go decision as well as to determine payback period (the amount of time needed for a project to pay for itself). The shorter the payback time, the more attractive the project from a financial viewpoint. This analysis also sets the stage for negotiations with vendors. This is a very important area, so a whole chapter has been dedicated to this topic (see Chapter 7).

- **Stakeholder Buy-in:** It is critical to go back to all the stakeholders and make sure that they have bought off on the proposed solution and confirm their role in the development of the solution to make it successful. Chapter 6 describes in detail how to achieve this.

- **Pilot Selection and Execution:** In a complex project such as RFID deployment, a pilot provides a great way to verify the validity of the technical and business architecture as well as gather additional data for fine-tuning the solution. The pilot should be designed to check critical elements of the solution. For example, an asset-tracking pilot might reveal that certain assets are hard to track because the tag is applied directly on a metallic surface or that the assets to be tracked are not getting close enough to the reader. Such issues can be fixed more easily if found early in the RFID project as opposed to later in the production system. The pilot may also bring out hardware, software, or architecture limitations that may need to be solved for a successful deployment. For these reasons, we advise you to structure the pilot as a closed loop system (within the four walls of an enterprise only) to exhibit better control over the environment. If interaction with a third party is critical in a pilot, the pilot should preferably be implemented in phases, with latter phases involving third parties (open loop system). When Sun Microsystems was conducting an RFID pilot in its manufacturing plant, it limited the scope to its internal systems only (closed loop system). The plant had to go through several trials and errors to find the optimal tag placement on various components such as server chassis and motherboards.

- **Detailed Business Plan:** The plan should document the decisions taken so far and lay out the future course of action. Specifically, it should clearly show the goal of the project, the business problem to be solved, the stakeholders, and the solution architecture. It should also highlight gaps in capabilities that need to be filled, as well as lay out marketing, deployment, and support plans.

- **Success Metrics:** No solution is complete if you can't tell whether it was successful in achieving its objectives. Development of the right type of metrics is critical in ensuring that the pertinent data and a process to capture it have been developed and implemented. For example, RFID deployment in a manufacturing operation should track specific improvement in supply chain operations such as inventory turnover or frequency of stock-outs. If a company only tracks read rates for RFID tagged items, but doesn't measure if better tracking enabled by RFID has increased inventory turnover, it can't determine whether the RFID project was successful in making the business operations more efficient. In such cases, the company may not be able to decide the right course of action for future investment in this area. The business architecture should support collection of such data. It is also imperative that after the suitable metrics are defined, the pilot results meet or exceed them. Failure to do so may signify a problem and require thorough review and update of several factors, including the pilot, project architecture, and risk mitigation plan. The definition of metrics varies by application and other considerations beyond the scope of this chapter. However, in general, a supply chain project measures metrics such as the rate of inventory turnover, the frequency of stock-outs, and the improvement in operating margins.

Typical questions to ask in this phase include the following:

- Is the technical architecture scalable and flexible enough to meet the company's business needs?

- Do you have the right business and organization infrastructure to enable this project? For example, are the stakeholders' goals aligned? Are rules of engagement and accountability established? Have the right business processes been set up to collect data?

- Does the cost-benefit analysis justify the project?

- What risks should you prepare for?
- Is the pilot structured in a way that its successful execution allows you to determine whether full-scale deployment can address key business needs of the company?
- How will you know whether this project was successful?
- Do you have a mechanism set up to roll out a pilot, and capture lessons learned?
- Have the stakeholders bought off on the proposed solution?
- Is the detailed business plan ready?

Avoid the following situations:

- A technical architecture that doesn't address issues such as investment protection
- Organization infrastructure considered as an afterthought
- No or inadequate risk mitigation plan
- No follow-through mechanism to measure the effectiveness of the pilot and act upon its results
- Success metrics that are so subjective they are impossible to quantify, measure, or compare

The output of this stage should consist of a well-defined and executed pilot, as well as a detailed solution implementation plan, including technical architecture, business analysis, and project measurement criteria. Feedback received from the pilot deployment should be incorporated in this plan. Special attention should be given to mitigation of project risk factors uncovered during the pilot.

Build and Deploy Solution

By now, you have identified the problem and a solution. The solution has even been tested as a proof of concept and the lessons learned from the exercise have been incorporated in the project plan. In this phase, the actual solution needs to be built and deployed. Proper execution of the plan developed earlier is extremely critical here. Roll-out of immature solutions without proper transition plans and follow-through can lead to system-wide failures. On the other hand, lack of leadership and strong execution skills can lead to a very slow roll-out, diminishing benefits and adding uncertainty throughout the enterprise.

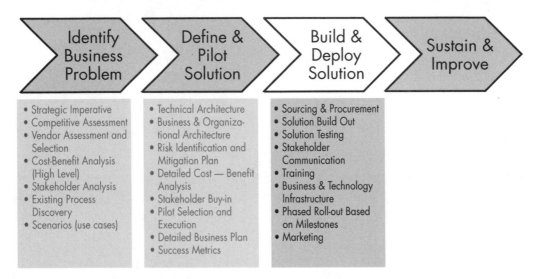

Identify Business Problem	Define & Pilot Solution	Build & Deploy Solution	Sustain & Improve
• Strategic Imperative • Competitive Assessment • Vendor Assessment and Selection • Cost-Benefit Analysis (High Level) • Stakeholder Analysis • Existing Process Discovery • Scenarios (use cases)	• Technical Architecture • Business & Organizational Architecture • Risk Identification and Mitigation Plan • Detailed Cost — Benefit Analysis • Stakeholder Buy-in • Pilot Selection and Execution • Detailed Business Plan • Success Metrics	• Sourcing & Procurement • Solution Build Out • Solution Testing • Stakeholder Communication • Training • Business & Technology Infrastructure • Phased Roll-out Based on Milestones • Marketing	

Key factors to consider in this phase are as follows:

- **Sourcing and Procurement:** Proper attention should be paid to sourcing and procurement of components to achieve steady supply and best prices. Because RFID deployments are expected to grow rapidly over the next several years, temporary shortages of tags may occur. To avoid getting hurt by such shortages, use the planning process as well as the pilot lessons to create as accurate a forecast of component needs as possible, so the orders can be placed in advance. Note that tag manufacturers are adding extra capacity, so the tag supply is not likely to be a constraint in the long run.

- **Solution Build-Out:** It is important to make sure that the deployment teams have the right resources, authority, and autonomy. The lessons learned from the pilot should be heavily leveraged. Project tracking should focus on deliverables as opposed to tasks. At pre-defined milestones, subject matter experts, end users, and management sponsors should perform project reviews to make sure that the solution meets the project guidelines and end-user requirements, as well as fits well with the strategic direction of the company. The U.S. Department of Defense (DoD), for example, had to ship 40,000 containers during the first Gulf War. Many of these contained redundant supplies due to the DoD's inability to locate the right supplies from a sea of containers. After the completion of the war, the DoD tested and found the RFID solution to meet its need of providing improved asset visibility. It has embarked on a phased solution build-out to deploy RFID in its operations. This has resulted in the creation of a network of RFID sensors (at the cost of $250M) that tracks more than 300,000 shipments per year using 1,300+ read/write stations in 800+ locations. Such massive solution build-out rests on the foundation of the original pilot carried out many years back, and other pilots carried out subsequently.

- **Solution Testing:** Testing should be performed at unit level as well as system level. Unit- or module-level testing is critical for testing architectural components. System-level testing is useful for testing usability and overall performance of the system. Teams consisting of end users and the project team should be involved in testing. For example, Wal-Mart tested its capability to receive RFID-equipped shipments with a handful of its top 100 suppliers for several months (system-level testing). As a result, several problems were identified, including trouble reading tagged objects containing liquid. Consequently, Wal-Mart relaxed its target requirement from 100% of the shipments tagged to approximately 65%. Imagine system-wide detection failures and delays in the Wal-Mart supply chain had it gone forward with its 100% compliance policy. Many pallets containing liquid-filled objects such as bottles of shampoo or detergent would not be read correctly, leading to delays across all of Wal-Mart's supply chain.

- **Stakeholder Communication:** Although the key stakeholders are usually involved in the project from its inception, the broader roll-out increases the number and presumably the types of stakeholders. Providing them with clear direction on what to expect at what point in time as well as clear transition and support plans is crucial. Using the original stakeholders as ambassadors in the organization can work well. When the DoD outlined its policy for use of RFID, it held several summits that its suppliers (stakeholders) could attend to find out more about the policy. In the summit, it invited several other suppliers who had long-standing RFID deployment projects to come as subject matter experts and share their experiences. Such a move can mean the difference between suppliers acting as partners with shared common goals versus acting as disinterested parties, or worse, adversaries. This topic is further explained in Chapter 6.

- **Training:** Enterprise-wide training is another critical factor to consider. Even the top management directives are sometimes interpreted by different employees in different ways. A training plan aimed at providing the right type of information to the right group of people can be critical in avoiding some of the variations in interpretation. The level of training required varies based on an employee's involvement in the project. For employees who are not directly related to the project, a short Web-based course or an instructional pamphlet should be sufficient. On the other hand, the employees directly responsible for execution should take extensive training with emphasis on troubleshooting and quality-control. In some cases, such as RFID deployment in supply chain, the training should even be rolled out to suppliers.

- **Business and Technology Infrastructure:** As mentioned earlier, IT alignment means that the right business and technology infrastructure is set up to execute a project. Testing should include how well the infrastructure can leverage the data provided by RFID systems and forward it on to various decision-making systems or individual reports for further processing and decision-making. When the DoD completed the build-out of its RFID sensor network (see Operation Iraqi Freedom / Operation Enduring Freedom (OEF/OIF) case study in Appendix A) and aligned its military (business) practices to leverage it, the results in terms of increased efficiency were impressive during the second Gulf War. Although the DoD deployed 30% fewer troops in the second war, it used 90% fewer shipping containers due to the improved supply chain visibility enabled by RFID.

- **Phased Roll-Out Based on Milestones:** As with any complex project, phased roll-out is critical. Things to watch are transition plans and implementation of lessons learned from previous phases into subsequent ones. Mid-course correction might be needed. As described earlier, teams with proper authority and autonomy are critical to achieve this.

- **Marketing:** The best IT deployment can fall short of its target if it is not leveraged in other functions of an organization. If the project was designed to improve a company's competitive position, the results and benefits of the project should be integrated into the company's marketing plan to gain customer mindshare and generate demand. The luxury carmaker Lexus does this effectively. Some Lexus cars come equipped with RFID-based lock and keys. As a result, a Lexus can "recognize" its owners. The company has leveraged this feature into its advertising. It positions this differentiation to further enhance the customer perception of Lexus as an innovator.

Typical questions to ask in this phase include the following:

- Do you have the right sourcing strategy to ensure adequate supplies at the right price?
- Is the current set of vendors helping you with investment protection?
- Do you have resources, including infrastructure, needed for an enterprise-wide solution build-out?
- Are milestones for the roll-out clearly defined and communicated?
- Have the solution testing and acceptance criteria been defined?
- Are the relevant people—for example, users and sustaining team—being trained? How is quality control ensured?
- Is the business benefit of this solution being integrated into marketing wherever appropriate?

Avoid the following situations:

- Inadequate focus on sourcing leading to short supply of parts or reengineering of solution
- Reliance on a favorite vendor that has little or no expertise with RFID
- Failed roll-out due to inadequate infrastructure
- Ad-hoc training of employees
- Stealth deployment of solution (no one knows about it or its benefits)

The output of this stage is a fully deployed solution that has been rolled out to the organization and marketed aggressively according to the plan. Proper stakeholder communications and training should be completed at this point.

Sustain and Improve

For many project teams involved in long and complex projects, a successful deployment may seem like the end of the project, but in reality, it is only the start of the project as far as external stakeholders, customers, and suppliers are concerned. Most of them are just beginning to experience the result of an RFID deployment, be it a new process, service, or product. At this stage, it is extremely critical to monitor and control the quality of the end-user or customer experience. The process or the solution should subsequently be optimized based on feedback.

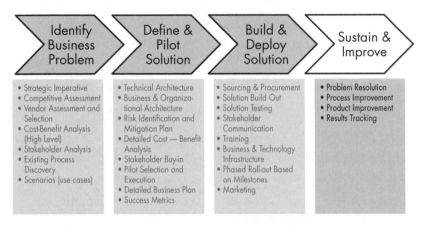

Key factors to consider in this phase are as follows:

- **Problem Resolution:** A dedicated team with some ties back to the original project drivers should be assembled to answer any questions by internal or external stakeholders (customers included) and resolve any problems that might come up.

- **Process Improvement:** Various forms of data collected, including performance metrics, comments, complaints, and surveys, should be analyzed to find common themes. This should help identify which process is working well and which needs improvement. The resulting knowledge should be fed back into the internal system for further use in process improvement or new service or process development.

- **Product Improvement:** Just as in process improvement, the results, new advances in the field, and standards should be evaluated to see if a solution redesign is warranted. For example, after the successful outcome of RFID deployment to track containers in the second Gulf war (see the OEF/OIF case study in Appendix A), the DoD decided to roll out RFID to track its supplies at a more granular level. It is hoping to derive significantly more savings and efficiencies from this expanded effort and is making investments to make it a success. To make the process more robust, it is also focusing on standardized architectures and encouraging various standards bodies to converge on common RFID communications standards. The latter focus is expected to help the whole industry move toward a better set of architectures based on open standards. This latest DoD initiative is described in more detail Chapter 9, "Mandates as Business Catalysts."

- **Results Tracking:** The metrics collected from the process roll-out should be reviewed with the management and other stakeholders at specified times, per business plan. This exercise helps determine how actual results compare to projections. The analysis of this data could not only indicate how well the original business issue is being addressed, but it may also point to areas of improvement in planning and forecasting.

Typical questions to ask in this phase include the following:

- Are the expected results being achieved? If not, what is the root cause analysis?
- How is the quality being ensured in areas such as solution delivery and issue resolution?
- Are customers satisfied? How likely are they to recommend your company?
- Are various data points and metrics being fed back into the system for process improvement?
- Is there a practical process improvement or upgrade path in place to sustain the project in the future?

Avoid the following situations:

- Customer dissatisfaction due to quality issues in the new product/service/process
- Feedback and metrics not being routed to the right organizations in charge of solution

The output of this stage is performance metrics as well as recommendations for improvement, which are fed back into the system for continuous improvement.

Knowledge Base

Organizational knowledge base, tacit and explicit, around the business issue or the process being addressed should be leveraged throughout an RFID deployment project. Hence, this part is shown separately from the four phases of the framework. It is not uncommon for the knowledge base to exist in several places, including databases, files, or even people's heads, without any clear links between these repositories. However, if leveraged properly, this knowledge can provide precious information about the context of the solution, in addition to the content (needed to develop the solution). Both are critical for the successful development of the solution.

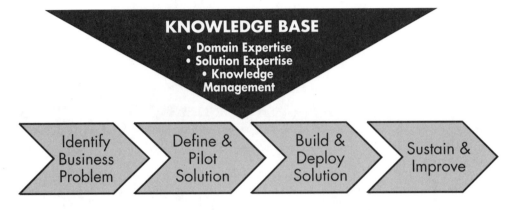

To make sure that the knowledge base is fully identified and leveraged, a knowledge map required to successfully carry out the project should be constructed at the beginning of the project. It should be compared against the inventory of the enterprise knowledge to identify project-specific knowledge gaps. A plan should be created to eliminate them. Top management or sponsors of the project should remain involved in this assessment and subsequent decisions such as determining whether to obtain the required knowledge through organic learning or outside help.

Typical questions to ask in this phase include the following:

- Have you identified the knowledge centers within your enterprise, pertaining to this problem?
- Are you effectively leveraging this knowledge base?
- Is the knowledge being gathered, stored, and distributed in a repeatable fashion for future use?

The output of this stage is an enterprise knowledge map, which accurately identifies its capabilities as well as centers of expertise.

The last piece of this framework is organizational mobilization. It deals with the "soft" skills of project management, such as motivating and aligning people to get results. It is a very important topic, to which we have dedicated the next chapter.

Summary

To the extent the decision to deploy an RFID solution is a business decision driven by a business need, the enterprise is likely to benefit more than if it were simply a decision to adopt a new technology. The deployment process itself can be quite complex, touching many parts of the organization. However, with the right plan, the deployment can yield significant benefits for the enterprise. The RFID deployment framework laid out in this chapter provides a guide for you to embark on this journey. Some of the pieces of the framework such as organizational mobilization and cost-benefit analysis are extensive and are further explained in subsequent chapters.

6

ORGANIZATIONAL MOBILIZATION

Five Questions This Chapter Will Answer

- How do I get my team to share my vision and goal for the project?
- What type of people should I enlist as supporters and how do I leverage them?
- How should I set the right expectations with my management team and leverage them effectively to achieve the project goals?
- What is the best way to deal with people who don't believe in this project or are putting up roadblocks?
- What are some examples of how others have done this?

In the previous chapter, we talked about the importance of looking at an RFID deployment in the broader context of the business problem being solved. The RFID deployment framework was introduced as a guide to enable this process. However, the process by itself is not sufficient. Unless there is a dedicated team behind the process who is working in unison to achieve the goal, the effort is not likely to be successful. Because an end-to-end RFID deployment is likely to touch various parts of an organization, such a team is likely to involve members from different parts of the organization, and possibly suppliers, partners, and customers. It is not easy to take such a diverse team, ensure that every team member has a clear understanding of the goal and his role in achieving it, and have each member work his best to achieve the goal. This requires complete organizational mobilization of stakeholders around the RFID deployment. In the previous chapter, we discussed how to identify the right stakeholders and what type of alignment to ensure between them. In this chapter, we will cover the following:

- Lay out how to achieve this alignment around an RFID deployment by expanding on the remaining piece of the RFID deployment framework and organizational mobilization.

- Provide real-world examples to clarify points.

> **Note:**
>
> Many of the examples provided in Chapter 5, "Framework for Deployment," this chapter, and Chapter 7, "Cost-Benefit Analysis," are derived from the real-life case studies based on interviews with industry practitioners like you. Details on some of these case studies are provided in Appendix A for your reference.

Achieving Organizational Mobilization

An RFID project likely touches many parts of an organization—from planning and sourcing to manufacturing and finance. It also touches many outside entities—from suppliers and partners to distribution agents and customers. It is critical that all these different entities, each with its own list of priorities, understand and commit to achieving the goals of the RFID deployment. Because such a deployment invariably involves a change in business processes, it is important to familiarize people with the required change and get their commitment for it.

How do you achieve organizational commitment (mobilization)? Through leadership, communication, and integration. The framework provides a structured way to do the following:

- Effectively communicate organizational priorities to individual team members and verify that the follow-up action plans are clear and specific

- Organize a team so that it is efficient in achieving the goal, yet flexible enough to find creative ways to achieve it

- Define and implement a realistic plan to successfully integrate the new process into existing business processes

Figure 6.1 shows the RFID deployment framework (introduced in the previous chapter) with emphasis on the organizational mobilization part. The part is broken into four pillars on which the total organizational commitment for an RFID project resides. In this chapter, we provide a set of questions that must be answered to successfully construct each pillar. We also mention several examples based on real-world situations to illustrate the points. Note that these questions and examples are samples only. They are likely to be different from one enterprise to the next. Nonetheless, they should provide a good starting point for you. We understand that there are countless books available on building and motivating teams that touch upon the mechanics and behavioral aspects of this issue. We are not trying to replicate that material in one chapter. Instead, we focus on those aspects of the organizational behavior that impact an RFID deployment the most.

The subsequent sections look at the framework in detail. The organizational mobilization achieved through this approach provides the commitment by the team members to work toward and achieve the common goal. The commitment can take many forms depending on the task required of the team members. Examples include taking an action to make a part of the deployment occur faster, providing public support, providing funding, or altering one's own goals and behavior. This commitment is essential for the cross-functional, cross-organizational team to carry out a successful RFID deployment.

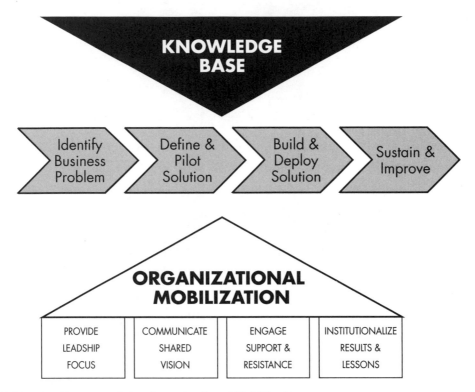

FIGURE 6.1   Framework for Organizational Mobilization

Provide Leadership Focus

Although all four pillars are important to gain organizational mobilization, the pillar of leadership focus is needed before others. Many people are usually apprehensive about a new commitment or a change, whether it involves changing an existing process to incorporate RFID technology or creating a new one from scratch centered around RFID. In such situations, a leader can provide the right vision, passion, drive, and resources. For example, a leader can help the team overcome its hesitation by taking on the responsibility for the outcome and assigning accountability to various stakeholders. He can also "evangelize" the cause of the team throughout the organization or to the broader customer and supplier community to get their acceptance for the RFID deployment when it does occur. He can also reinforce these points by modeling his own actions around the goals.

Typically, a leader has the authority to make decisions, allocate resources, and hold people accountable for their actions. Usually, the executive team or senior management gives him such authority. Although this is critical, it is not sufficient. A leader should also be a motivator, a change agent, and a role model by behavior. Many leaders posses all these qualities, but it is not a requirement. Many times, teams have a formal leader with the right authority and one or more informal leaders. The informal leaders influence the rest of the team to accept the change. In many cases, these leaders are also thought leaders, finding creative ways to solve problems and cutting through the dissent to find common grounds for progress. It is critical for the formal leader to recognize and nurture such informal leaders.

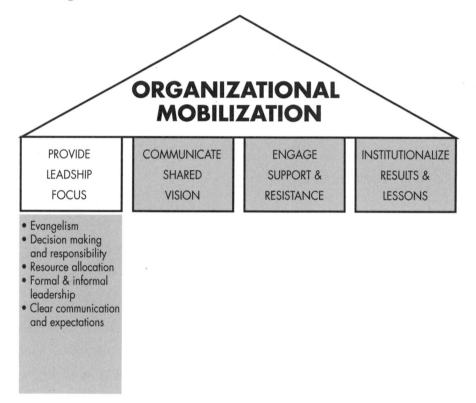

Whether formal or informal leadership, the leader must avoid certain common pitfalls. For example, the leader should show visible support for the team at the right time. Lack of such active leadership can prompt external stakeholders to not take the team seriously. This, in turn, can prompt the team to stay on the sidelines and not take initiative or risks. Another common pitfall is a lengthy and confusing decision-making process. With the RFID standards still evolving and companies worried about investment protection, the decision to select a vendor or a technology should be clearly communicated to the team. Lacking this, the team may question the leader's commitment to the end goal, hurting creativity and follow-through.

In addition to providing focus for the team, the leader must communicate effectively and set the right expectations with his superiors and other sponsors of the RFID project. The definition of mutual deliverables should be a part of this communication. For example, the executive sponsor can keep the rest of the executive team apprised of the status of the project and get team support for cross-organizational resource commitment to the project, whereas the leader keeps the project on track.

Typical questions to address to construct this pillar include the following:

- How will team members, superiors, and other internal and external stakeholders know that the leadership focus is appropriate?
- What individual actions are needed to carry out the vision?
- Are the right stakeholders committing to the goals through actions and resources?
- How can it be determined if individuals in the team are acting as informal leaders and taking initiative to make the project a success?
- What other leaders need to get involved in support of the project?
- Do team members understand the benefits and opportunities of deploying an RFID solution?

Communicate Shared Vision

The goals and the desired result of an RFID project, whether it is total supply chain visibility or better asset tracking, must be expressed to the whole team in a clear manner such that it generates energy and inspires the team to commit. The objective is to paint a picture in team members' minds so that they can see what the end-state looks like and see themselves in the future. That is considered a *shared vision*.

Communicating this shared vision to all the team members is critical in successfully convincing the team to achieve the goal. The vision becomes truly shared when the team members feel ownership of the vision. At that point, the team becomes an example of organizational mobilization. Likewise, repeat communication about the shared vision is critical in making sure everyone is on-board with the business priorities. It is important to periodically check to see if stakeholders can articulate the same picture of the future shared state. Because achievement of the shared vision requires resources, it is important to ensure that the resource requirements are understood.

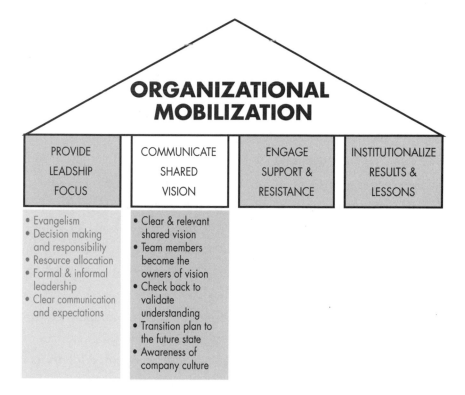

Wal-Mart and the DoD are doing this with their extended team (suppliers) by holding summits for the suppliers, understanding the issues facing them and even adjusting the vision based on those issues (see Chapter 9, "Mandates as Business Catalysts").

If the shared vision is not communicated properly, it can lead to sub-optimal results. For example, if the team is not aligned with what the future state looks like, it is harder to convince someone to stay with the project through rough patches. An unclear or under-communicated vision can confuse people and increase their resistance to the RFID deployment.

Another element to focus on in this stage is the transition path from the current state to the future one. Although team members may agree on the shared vision, the difficulties encountered in transitioning from the current to the future state may take them by surprise, resulting in a loss of initiative and teamwork when they are needed the most. For example, a consumer goods company moving from a barcode-based tracking system to a partial RFID-based tracking system (case and pallet level only, no item level) may have to sustain two systems for a significant period of time—one to read barcodes and the other to read RFID tags. In addition, fine-tuning the system to get accurate tracking of RFID-enabled packages may temporarily disrupt other operations or require diverting resources to the RFID pilot. This process is likely to increase quantity and complexity of the work performed by the operations staff.

In addition, team members will see new activities affecting their daily work environment. Some of them may seem unrelated as they may not be able to tie each of the activities to the RFID project or understand the rationale for them. If they are not prepared for the increased workload, complexity, or added confusion, they are likely to see the project as "taking too long" or "not being as useful," and not give it their best.

There are two things a team can do to mitigate this problem: address the context for change and account for the culture when making the plans. Showing people the context for change, whether it is market demand, regulations, or competitive pressure, and explaining to them how internal resources may be reallocated can help minimize their concerns during the transition period when many, seemingly unrelated, activities happen simultaneously.

Focus on company culture is equally important. Some company cultures are more open to change than others. Some work best when the process change or process introduction is instigated from upper management, as opposed to others where grass roots initiatives work most effectively. Depending on the cultural dynamics, the team may have to make sure the right people are supporting the RFID deployment and showing the right type of support at various levels of the organization.

Typical questions to address to construct this pillar include the following:

- Is the shared vision compelling and understood well enough to create enthusiasm in the team?

- Can the team members describe the shared future state?

- What is being done to make sure that the vision is shared by key internal or external stakeholders?

- Is the rationale for the project clear to the appropriate stakeholders, including how it affects them? Have steps been taken to mitigate their concerns?

- Is there a mechanism in place so that others can provide feedback and suggestions for improvements? Is there a way to systematically address them and communicate back the results?

Engage Support and Resistance

As in any large project, the team is likely to encounter some stakeholders who are supportive, some who are neutral, and some who are resistant to the project. A typical project adoption curve is shown in Figure 6.2.

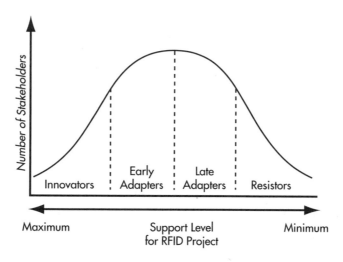

FIGURE 6.2 Project Adoption Curve

The *innovators* and *early adopters* are usually supportive of the project and willing to help make it a success. The *late adopters* are cautious and sometimes wary of the project. However, with the right proof points, they can be converted into supporters over time. Even when they are not supportive of the project, they are usually not against it. *The resisters*, on the other hand, are the stakeholders who don't like the project for a variety of reasons. Some may not believe in it, whereas others may stand to lose something because of the project. Not only do they not support the project, but some may actively work against it. For example, a shop floor worker responsible for manually checking the barcodes on pallets and cases going out of the facility might see the RFID deployment as a threat to job security. If you can leverage supporters to further the project and convert the resisters into supporters or contain their negative actions, the project is likely to move forward faster. Failure to do so can result in the project not being successful. In the preceding example, the shop floor worker might be educated about RFID and provided options to focus on other activities, hence reducing his anxiety about job security.

How do you handle these different types of stakeholders? By building partnerships with them. The key to success here is to seek out resistance, understand the opposing viewpoint, and find a common ground for constructive engagement. Two-way communication is essential. At the same time, do not use supporters to unduly force the resisters. It is important to note that a stakeholder raising a concern is not necessarily a resister. The team may find out that the shop floor worker in the preceding example has a valid concern about the practicality of the RFID deployment when reading tags on liquid bottles. Addressing such valid concerns will likely make the deployment more successful. The following steps can help convert a resister:

- Advocate your position—the rationale for the project and how it can benefit them. Let them know that their input is essential for success.

- Inquire about the resister's concerns by asking open-ended questions. This helps you understand not only the stated concern but also the context behind it. Use intuition and other background information to get to the root cause behind a stated position.

- Summarize what was heard to let the resister know he was heard correctly.

- Lay out suggestions that might address the resister's concerns or a course of action that can address his concerns in a timely manner. Specify what you, as a leader, expect from him. A phased approach to building partnership where you first engage the resister in smaller, easier tasks might work better.

- Always leave the meeting with identified next steps and a reason to meet again after a defined period.

Successful engagement may result in the resisters becoming supporters. In many cases, their insight can alter the course of a project to make it better or more robust. At the same time, you should be cognizant not to spend so much time converting resisters to the point that you lose sight of the goal, or worse, lose time and supporters.

The preceding steps can also be used to help turn neutral stakeholders into supporters. Another consideration for the neutrals is a well-defined project value proposition. Often, they are not clear about what benefit the project brings to them and what their role in the project is. Crafting the right value proposition can help convert them into supporters. For example, a store's stocking clerk may view addition of Smart Shelves (see Chapter 1, "A Better Way of Doing Things") in the store as an unnecessary introduction of technology. If the team conveys the benefit of this technology—less manual checking of shelves—the clerk may become a supporter. He may even have some suggestions on how to position the antennae around the shelves to improve accuracy.

> ### Typical questions to address to construct this pillar include the following:
>
> - Have the supporters as well as the resisters been engaged and heard?
> - Is the rationale behind their resistance and how to address it understood?
> - Is there a plan to leverage support and engage resistance?
> - Has the right value proposition been conveyed to the neutral stakeholders to convert them into adopters?

Institutionalize Results and Lessons

After an RFID project has been successfully deployed in one part of the organization, as a pilot or as a small-scale solution, the next step typically involves an organization-wide roll-out and sustenance. This changes the project dynamics. Whereas a small, focused team worked on the project before, a much larger team consisting of new members starts to work on the bigger project now. Whereas the knowledge base residing in the smaller team was leveraged through informal mechanisms before, the informal mechanisms need to be replaced by the formal ones so the larger team can tap into the knowledge base now. The number of stakeholders also increases. Some of the older stakeholders may move on to work in other areas. Although an obvious solution to the situation is to make sure that the results and the lessons learned are captured (as discussed in Chapter 5), it is not sufficient. That solution just addresses the mechanical aspect of project sustenance. To make the solution lasting, the results and the change must be built into the organization, that is, institutionalized. When a new process or a new way of doing business through RFID is institutionalized, it has a much higher chance of surviving the departure of the old team, changes in the business climate, or even changes in the technology.

However, the process of institutionalization is not easy. Even the most seasoned project teams often make a mistake in this step. Why? Because this step requires a slightly different set of skills to succeed. For example, the team testing out an RFID deployment on the factory floor under a tight deadline is likely to improvise, overcome resistance by finding temporary solutions, and do whatever it takes to get the project completed. When the project is completed and the time for a company-wide roll-out arrives, a different type of approach is required. Now, the team needs to bring new members on board, identify and address organizational interdependencies on a much larger scale than before, and most importantly, figure out how to share lessons learned with a wider, more diverse organization in a language that is understood by many.

To institutionalize the results, it is important to make sure that the right types of people with the right types of capabilities are on-board to take the project forward. The goals should be set up to encourage people to follow through and commit to the on-going success of the project. Lastly, the right type of organizational structure should be set up with people or a team having clear responsibility and resources to carry the project forward.

Typical questions to address to construct this pillar include the following:

- Are the people with the right capability being recruited to the team for the larger roll-out? Do they clearly understand what is expected of them?

- Are the (mechanical) systems set up to capture and share the knowledge base?

- Are some core team members from the original team going to stay over and oversee the institutionalization of the project?

- Is the upper management supportive of the wider roll-out? Are they doing a follow-through to overcome obstacles such as organizational boundaries?

- Are the right metrics set up for the company-wide project roll-out? Does a process exist to measure and analyze them to make better business decisions?

Summary

The human factor is very important to consider in an RFID deployment project, especially because such a project is likely to touch many internal and external groups. The key to success here is to mobilize this large stakeholder base to focus on achieving the deployment goals. The four pillars (phases) of organizational mobilization—provide leadership focus, communicate shared vision, engage support and resistance, and institutionalize results and lessons—can help you enlist support and mobilize it to achieve your goals. In the next two chapters, we focus on the two specific aspects of the RFID deployment framework: cost-benefit analysis and vendor considerations.

7

COST-BENEFIT
ANALYSIS

Five Questions This Chapter Will Answer

- What types of benefits can an RFID project provide?
- How do I create a holistic business case for RFID that balances long- and short-term investments and benefits?
- What elements should I include in my cost-benefit analysis?
- Are there some guidelines (characterizations of cost-benefit) for certain applications?
- Which costs are one-time, and which ones are recurring?

The last two chapters showed how to evaluate RFID deployments in the context of real business problems, and why a dedicated team is needed to ensure successful deployment of RFID. A framework was introduced to provide a practical approach to address these issues. In this chapter, we expand on another consideration critical to a successful RFID deployment: cost-benefit analysis.

> **Note:**
>
> Many of the examples provided in Chapter 5, "Framework for Deployment," Chapter 6, "Organizational Mobilization," and this chapter are derived from the real-life case studies based on interviews with industry practitioners like you. Details on some of these case studies are provided in Appendix A for your reference.

Because the decision to deploy RFID technology in an enterprise is a business decision and not a technology decision, cost-benefit analysis is a key component of this decision. If an RFID deployment cannot be justified in terms of its economic value to the company, it is not likely to help the company; and consequently, it is not likely to remain a viable deployment over the long term. Although the mandates such as the ones issued by Wal-Mart or the U.S. Department of Defense (DoD) require various suppliers to use RFID tags, unless a supplier can figure out how this can be leveraged in its business to improve profit and increase capacity utilization, the net benefit to the supplier can be mediocre or even negative in the long term. Cost-benefit analysis can help a supplier analyze the impact of an RFID project on its business. Based on the analysis, a supplier can make a go/no-go decision, structure the project in a way to capture immediate benefits first (low-hanging fruit), or even modify the scope of the project to maximize benefits. For example, a supplier complying with the Wal-Mart mandate might leverage the same RFID infrastructure in its dealings with other customers (see Chapter 9, "Mandates as Business Catalysts," for a list of other selected mandates) or its own suppliers. This could result in a more timely delivery to its customers or better inventory control of its own supplies. Such moves could increase the benefit of an RFID deployment significantly, making the overall project more attractive.

Many factors play a role in determining RFID technology's costs and benefits. For example, costs can be fixed, such as investment in new tools and processes to install and test tags, or recurring, such as the cost of RFID tags or the cost associated with applying them on cases and testing them. Benefits can be direct, such as reduction in shrinkage and buffer stock, or indirect, such as better customer service due to more detailed and accurate understanding of ship time and date of arrival. In the next several sections, we do the following:

- Illustrate what type of benefits a company should look forward to and how various components of an RFID deployment can drive overall project costs.

- Characterize several RFID deployment examples in terms of cost-benefit.

Analyzing Benefits

Benefits of an RFID deployment can be categorized based on time (short-term versus long-term benefits) or tangibility (direct versus indirect). In some cases, such as tagging of cattle or item-level tagging in an end-to-end supply chain application, a *network effect* may also be present; the value of an RFID deployment may be minimal when only a few participants (cattle producers or suppliers) deploy RFID. However, the value increases significantly when the majority of the participants (including upstream and downstream producers in some cases) deploy RFID and the data is shared among the participants.

Types of Benefits

We classify the benefits of RFID deployment in a matrix in Figure 7.1. For each quadrant of the matrix, a sample list of applications that fit the characteristics of that quadrant is also provided. Some applications may provide both types of benefits: direct and indirect, or long term and short term. Some applications may even move from one quadrant to another based on changes in regulatory, competitive, or other drivers. For example, in the United States, federal subsidies for cattle owners to tag their cattle will move the cattle tagging applications' benefit realization from the long-term timeframe to the short-term.

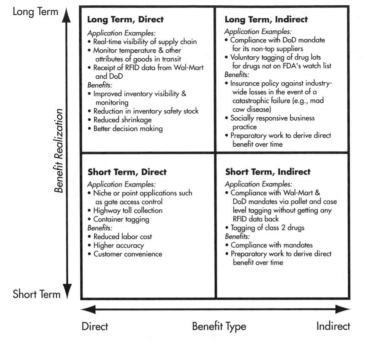

FIGURE 7.1   Benefits of an RFID Deployment

From Figure 7.1, you might deduce that the place to be is the left-hand side of the matrix (direct benefits), preferably the lower-left quadrant where the benefits are immediately monetized. However, many RFID deployments do not fall in this area. Some that are long term or exhibit indirect benefit will, over time, move to the lower-left quadrant. In this scenario, it is not advisable to rule out a project just because it doesn't provide short-term direct benefits.

However, the question remains: How would a company correctly evaluate what level of overall benefits justify their deployment? To answer this, you need to evaluate additional factors, described in the following section.

Finding the Right Benefit Level

In addition to looking at the type of RFID application and its benefits, a company also needs to look at its business environment and its organizational readiness for innovation to make the right cost-benefit decision. Because the specifics of these two factors vary from company to company, we have provided examples to further clarify this point.

A company that is under pressure from its customers or regulatory bodies to comply with a certain mandate may have to deploy RFID in its operations, or risk losing business or face a penalty. Many of Wal-Mart and DoD suppliers fall in this area. Such companies derive indirect benefits from the deployment. Companies in this situation should work with customers and suppliers to figure out how to use the data collected from such deployments in other business operations to gain direct benefits. For example, a cereal manufacturer could use the inventory data coming back from Wal-Mart to make its upstream purchase decisions. A cattle manufacturer responding to an RFID tag law (see the Michigan Department of Agriculture case study in Appendix A) for the cattle may use the audited pedigree data to break into new markets, selling "traceable" meat and thereby minimizing the consumers' health concerns. Such deployment can benefit the industry as a whole as well, because the overall quality of the food supply is enhanced.

A company whose organizational readiness for innovation is high can use RFID to gain competitive advantage, even if the benefits of the specific application are not short term. Wal-Mart is a good example. It has a history of using technology (for example, barcode) to improve its operations and gain competitive advantage. Naturally, it is also one of the early adopters of RFID technology.

In some situations, a company may decide to deploy RFID even if the benefits are indirect or long term. RFID use in healthcare organizations to deliver the right medicine to the right patient fits in this category. On the surface, the direct benefits of improved productivity seem to be minor. However, the indirect benefits seem pretty compelling considering that the wrong medicine can potentially kill a patient. It is estimated that more than 7,000 patients die every year in hospitals due to medication errors,[1] and many more suffer adverse reactions. If RFID deployment can curtail this number, not to mention reduction in lawsuits against the hospitals, the cost-benefit trade-off may be worthwhile for a healthcare organization, even though the benefits are indirect and long term.

A company that can reap direct benefits from RFID deployment in the short term may have a different consideration. In this case, the reason to deploy RFID is straightforward, but the time to deployment may be a factor. If such a company wants to delay the deployment due to its IT readiness, it may have to rethink that decision because of competitive pressure. A 3PL (third-party logistics) company that distributes goods to retailers is a good example. It can use RFID in place of barcode scanners to reap direct benefits in labor cost and accuracy. Barcodes on various pallets at

---

[1] "To Err is Human: Building a Safer Health System," Institute of Medicine, November 1999.

such facilities are usually scanned manually. If a pallet is not oriented correctly, a physical move may be required to read the code. A forklift equipped with an RFID reader can read all such pallets. This not only saves time, but also adds accuracy. Strategically placed readers can detect the movement of pallets throughout the warehouse, significantly reducing the number of items that are lost due to misplacement or shrinkage. The 3PL provider may have to invest in the RFID gear, but if it doesn't make the investment, one of its competitors might. Such pressure will likely force these organizations to deploy RFID.

Calculation of the benefits due to RFID deployment requires looking at savings across the overall business process and not just one part of it. Many times, proper calculation requires breaking down the result into its components. The Smart & Secure Tradelanes case study in Appendix A provides a good example. In this case, the benefits from tracking containers as they travel across the sea come from better supply chain visibility (in addition to indirect benefits such as security and compliance with regulations). However, to calculate the benefits, you need to break "better supply chain visibility" into its components such as reduction in safety stock (benefit equivalent to 0.25% to 0.30% of the cost of goods), reduction in (inventory) pipeline (0.13% to 0.16%), reduction in service charges (0.08% to 0.10%), administrative savings (0.04% to 0.05%), and reduction in pilferage/loss (0.04% to 0.05%). The combined benefits: a savings reaching 0.54% to 0.66% of the cost of the goods in an average container.

It is important to keep in mind, though, that benefits address only one aspect of the RFID deployment decision. The other aspect is cost. Although the benefit levels mentioned in the preceding example implicitly address costs, it is important for a decision maker to do the next level of cost analysis.

Elements of Cost

The cost of an RFID deployment can be broken down among three key areas: hardware, software, and services. Hardware costs include the cost of tags, readers, antennae, host computers, and network equipment (cables, routers, and so on). Software costs include the cost of creation or upgrade of middleware and other applications (for example, ERP and SCM). Service costs include the cost of installation, tuning, integration of various components, training, support and maintenance, and business process reengineering (workflow).

Tags

Tag costs are one of the key considerations in an RFID deployment. Tags come in various shapes and sizes based on applications. These factors affect tag pricing significantly. Other factors such as range, on-board memory, read/write capability, and active/passive configuration also impact the cost of tags. Generally, application requirement is the primary driver for the selection of a particular type of tag. Two types of costs are associated with tags: acquisition cost and preparation cost. Also note that some of these costs are recurring costs, so careful planning and negotiation can bring volume discounts, lowering the costs. Because tag prices are coming down over time, you should consider buying tags in phases for a large, multi-phase project to take advantage of lower spot prices in the future.

Acquisition Costs

The Electronic Product Code (EPC) passive UHF tags typically cost around 40 cents. Significant volumes in hundreds of millions, however, yield deep discounts on these prices. Based on projected tag volumes as well as projected improvements in processes used to make such tags, the price of such a passive UHF tag is expected to fall anywhere from 5 cents to 15 cents in the next several years. The tag price between 5 to 10 cents is likely to act as a catalyst for widespread adoption of RFID tags for item-level tagging in retail and supply chain areas.

Other non-EPC tags vary in prices. Passive tags used in the cattle industry cost around $2. Tags used in access control typically are quite small with very short range measured in inches. These tags cost in tens of cents (packaging, such as embedding the tag in a card the size of a credit card, is extra). Active tags, on the other hand, have long range and their own power supply. Such tags can cost up to $100 or more. Special purpose tags designed for a specific application can cost up to $100 or more. These tags typically exhibit special features (for example, the capability to withstand very high temperature, pressure, or concentration of corrosive materials) not available in mass volume tags. Semi-passive (or semi-active) tags can cost anywhere from a few dollars in small quantities to tens of cents in volume.

Preparation Costs

Tag acquisition costs are not the only costs driving the overall cost of a tag in a deployment. You must factor in related costs as well. For example, if a tag is printed on a label, the cost of the RFID label printer/encoder should be factored in. A 3PL logistics vendor or a large CPG (Consumer Packaged Goods) manufacturer would need manual labor or an applicator machine to apply tags to the boxes it ships. Mounting tags on a metal surface or a container filled with liquid may require special mounting accessories so the tag can be read properly by a reader. When in an industrial environment such as auto assembly, the tag may need to be packed in heat resistant packaging. Depending on your situation, some of these preparation costs should be factored into tag costs.

Readers

Reader range, multifrequency handling capability (agile readers), and antennae capability affect reader costs. A typical reader comes with a set of APIs (application programming interfaces) to communicate data with upstream processing elements such as a host computer running the middleware or other applications. Some manufacturers combine a host computer and readers in one package to create a reader appliance. The price varies from several hundred dollars to more than $5,000 for readers used in rugged industrial environments. Handheld readers typically combine the antenna and the reader in one package, costing more than $500 in volume. The cost of mounting readers and antennae (for example, to build a reader/antennae portal) should also be factored in cost-benefit calculations.

Antennae

There are two sets of antennae in an RFID deployment: one connected to the RFID chip and one connected to the reader. Some readers may have multiple antennae connected to them. The one connected to the chip is considered a part of the tag and is not addressed here.

Several types of antennae (connected to the reader) are available with different size, range, and directional output. Sometimes, aesthetic or functional considerations may require design of a special antenna. An EPC-compliant antenna costs up to $500. Price of a non-EPC antenna varies from tens of dollars to several hundred dollars, depending on the application.

Host Computer, Middleware, and Host Applications

The host computer typically runs the RFID middleware software, and in some cases, other applications such as inventory management and asset tracking. If it is just running the RFID middleware, it could be a small server costing $2000 or more. If it is a larger machine that is used to run other applications, it may cost tens of thousands of dollars. If your company already has such a setup, you don't necessarily need to incur this cost. Some vendors also package RFID middleware with a host computer, making it an RFID middleware appliance. Such appliances provide out-of-the-box functionality and manageability, making them ideal for facilities that don't have extensive resources to set up and manage a host computer system. Rugged versions of a host computer can cost anywhere from 20% to 100% more than the cost of a comparable base model.

The cost of RFID middleware could be anywhere from $25,000 to $100,000 and include a site license. The RFID middleware appliance could cost from $8,000 to $20,000 per device. The cost of application software depends on the application.

Installation

Installation of all these components—tags, readers, antennae, host computers, and related network infrastructure (for example, switches and cables)—can be complicated. In a retail environment, some of the elements such as readers and antennae may need to be concealed or made less conspicuous for aesthetic reasons. In warehouses, new power connections and other network cabling might need to be provided to install readers, antennae, and host computers in various parts of the warehouse. Depending on the environment, additional gear may be required to set up a network, whether it is wired Ethernet or Wi-Fi (Wireless Fidelity). Depending on the size of the project, cabling costs (CAT5 or others) can also be substantial. In the cattle industry, readers installed in the slaughter facilities need to be protected so they aren't damaged by the cattle accidentally bumping into them. Each environment has its own unique set of challenges, along with some common ones. An experienced system integrator is essential here. Numerous service companies do this type of work. Some specialize specifically in RFID installations. More details can be found in Chapter 8, "Vendor Considerations and Landscape," and the book's companion Web site, *www.rfidfieldguide.com*.

Tuning

Tuning plays a critical role in successful implementation of an RFID application. It refers to activities such as tag/reader placement or shielding to get optimum performance. Because an RFID application is based on radio waves, disturbance (noise) from other devices that utilize radio waves can affect the network performance, that is, accurate read and write of tags. Many devices we use today—for example, motors in a manufacturing plant—or many elements we encounter widely—for example, liquid and metal—can affect RF performance. An RF signal sent by a reader may not be equally powerful in all directions or may have certain "blind" spots where RF energy is quite low. Hence, the RFID system may need to be tuned by an experienced RF engineer. The engineer can tune reader and antennae for specific situations or use shielding to block RF noise emitting from other devices. Tuning requirements can vary by environment. In healthcare facilities, the disturbance comes not from motors but from patient monitoring devices. Only certain frequencies, typically in the HF (High Frequency) band can be used in this environment.

Integration and Business Process Reengineering

Full benefits of an RFID deployment can only be realized when the data collected from various tagged objects is used for better decision-making. This can lead to increased profit or operations that are more streamlined. Depending on the type of application an RFID system needs to interface with, the cost can vary significantly. It is usually easier to integrate with Web-based applications that run on standards-based middleware (for example, J2EE application server or Web server). On the other hand, legacy applications with proprietary interfaces may require more integration. In some cases, the integration project may require overall rearchitecting of the network as well as other business processes, going into the realm of business process reengineering. Initial design, programming, and integration costs such as those associated with encoding unique product IDs onto tags (serialization) as well as updating and verifying shared databases with tag data (synchronization) are part of the integration costs. Subsequently, these costs are also incurred for ongoing maintenance of the projects.

Support and Maintenance

The on-going support and maintenance of RFID applications and reevaluation of existing processes to maximize the usage of newly available data represent additional costs as well. For example, a software support and service agreement can annually cost up to 15% of software license cost. Physical equipment can depreciate or fail altogether and need replacement. Various existing processes may need to be re-engineered to take advantage of the real-time data collected by an RFID system. Different stakeholders may need to be trained on how to use these new processes. Such costs should be factored into the planning and cost-benefit analysis to create a comprehensive picture of the RFID deployment.

Cost-Benefit Characterization of Selected Applications

In this section, we use the drivers mentioned thus far to characterize selected applications in terms of cost-benefit. Because some of the costs vary based on specific situations, we have provided relative costs of components as opposed to absolute costs.

As already mentioned, a cost-benefit analysis of an RFID deployment depends on several factors. Because the importance of these factors depends on the specific application being considered, it is not possible to provide a simple cost-benefit formula that is universally applicable. Instead, we take a sample of RFID applications from Chapter 1, "A Better Way of Doing Things," and discuss which cost drivers are critical for them based on their inherent characteristics. You can utilize this data in two ways. In some cases, your application may be exactly what is described in here. In that case, you can use this characterization as a guide to further build cost-benefit scenarios. In the case where your application is different from what is being described here, you can find the closest match and modify it to build cost-benefit scenarios. In addition, you can use the illustrated example provided in the Smart & Secure Tradelanes case study (Appendix A) as a guide to build a cost-benefit scenario.

> **Note:**
>
> The Key Benefits are taken from the four primary benefits outlined in Chapter 1. In cases where an application provides multiple benefits, the primary benefit is considered the Key Benefit.

TABLE 7.1   Cost-Benefit Characterization of Selected Applications

Key Benefit: Security and Authentication			
Application	**Characteristics**	**Cost Drivers**	**Comments**
Electronic Article Surveillance	• Prevents shoplifting through inexpensive 1-bit tags • Closed loop system that doesn't interact with other systems • Low or High Frequency tags with range < 3 ft	• Primary ($$): Installation, 1-bit tags • Secondary ($): Tags, Readers, Training	• In widespread deployment now
Document Authentication	• Establishes authenticity of a document through an embedded RFID chip • Special tags embedded in the paper • Can use read-only or read-write tags	• Primary ($$): Tagged paper, Integration with other systems to establish authenticity Business Process Re-engineering • Secondary ($): Readers, Training, Installation	• Mid-term (12–36 months) timeframe for general deployment; requires technology and pricing maturity • Customer education and acceptance key to success
Access Control	• Tags embedded in badges or key-chains can provide access to restricted facilities • Closed loop system that may interact with the directory infrastructure of the enterprise to provision and revoke access on the fly • Low frequency tags with range < 6 inches	• Primary ($$): Tags and readers, integration of tag data with back-end directory infrastructure • Secondary ($$): Readers, maintenance, installation	• In widespread deployment now • Smart tags that can also store other keys and passwords, and can act as multiple access device are gaining popularity
Electronic Drug Pedigree	• Prevent proliferation of counterfeit drugs by keeping a record of a drug's pedigree as it moves through supply chain • Open loop system that requires some type of central repository to store drug pedigree information • Ultra High or Microwave frequency passive tags with range > 3 feet	• Primary ($$): Tags, Integration with central repository, Training and Process Re-engineering • Secondary ($$): Installation of tags on cases and at item level	• Mid-term (12–36 months) timeframe for general deployment; requires technology and pricing maturity • Customer education and acceptance key to success

TABLE 7.1 continued

Key Benefit: Safety			
Application	**Characteristics**	**Cost Drivers**	**Comments**
People Monitoring	• Help locate missing or lost kids in amusement parks • Help locate and track whereabouts of the elderly in senior care facilities • Active or semi active tags more likely, passive UHF tags in some applications	• Primary ($$): Readers, Installation and Integration, Process Re-engineering • Secondary ($): Tags	• Near term (< 12 months) timeframe for general deployment since direct benefits and technology available today • Operational in some amusement parks already
Patient Care	• Provide patient safety and id the newborns • Accurately identify the patient for a surgical procedure or for drug administration • Mainly HF tags	• Primary ($$): Integration, Maintenance, Process Reengineering • Secondary ($): Tags, Readers	• Mid term (12-36 months) timeframe for general deployment • Requires technology maturity, and patient education
Environment Sensing and Monitoring	• Monitor environmental conditions such as temperature for perishable items • Identify tampering with items such as food, drugs • Active or passive tags with sensory capabilities	• Primary ($$): Tags, Integration and Monitoring • Secondary ($): Readers	• Mid term (12-36 months) timeframe for general deployment • Requires technology maturity, supplier acceptance and process re-engineering

Key Benefit: Convenience			
Application	**Characteristics**	**Cost Drivers**	**Comments**
Crowd Control	• Provide means to process guests / visitors faster at concerts or night clubs • HF (High Frequency) tags, injectable tags in some cases • Closed loop system	• Primary ($$): Tags, Process Re-engineering, Installation • Secondary ($): Readers	• Mid term (12 36 months) timeframe for general deployment
Payment	• RFID based smart cards can act as e-wallets, allowing consumers to pay using the card • HF (High Frequency) tags used in this closed loop system	• Primary ($$): Tags, Cards, Infrastructure, Process Re-engineering	• Mid term (12–36 months) timeframe for general deployment

TABLE 7.1   continued

Key Benefit: Process Efficiency			
Application	**Characteristics**	**Cost Drivers**	**Comments**
Industrial Automation	• Automate the process of assembling various components through use of RFID to verify components and assembly instructions • Closed loop system	• Primary ($$): Tags, Integration • Secondary ($): Readers	• In use today; continues to improve and gain popularity
Track and Trace / Supply Chain Integration	• Likely to be the most prevalent use of RFID in supply chain • Used in functions such as bar code replacement, compliance with mandates, supply chain visibility • Use of passive UHF tags in most cases, with range > 3 feet • Primary application of EPC defined standards	• Primary ($$): Tags, Integration, Installation, Process Re-engineering • Secondary ($): Maintenance	• Track and Trace: Near term (< 12 months) timeframe for general deployment due to various mandates • End-to-end Supply Chain Integration can take 2–5 years • Tag pricing and read accuracy key performance factors affecting wide-spread rollout • Open loop system that interacts with various business applications

Summary

Cost-benefit analysis is critical to the successful deployment of an RFID project. If an RFID project cannot be evaluated in terms of its potential benefits to the company, and if those benefits don't exceed the benefit threshold required, the solution is not likely viable in the long term. The benefits of an RFID project can be direct or indirect, long term or short term. As shown in the chapter, the pricing of RFID components varies based on the solution type. A sample cost-benefit characterization of some of the key applications provides you with a tool to develop your own cost-benefit analysis. In the next chapter, we describe what to look for in vendors, and how to evaluate them.

8

VENDOR CONSIDERATIONS AND LANDSCAPE

Five Questions This Chapter Will Answer

- How should I evaluate the capabilities of various vendors?
- How do I select a trusted advisor for the RFID project I am considering?
- How can I accelerate the implementation and deployment of my RFID project?
- What is the role of computer systems vendors in RFID projects?
- Where can I find a comprehensive RFID vendor list?

In this chapter, we conclude the framework we started in Chapter 5, "Framework for Deployment," to show you how to deploy RFID in your enterprise and what factors to consider. The vendor selection process is the last element of the framework for which we provide details. Proper vendor selection often makes the difference between a successful project and a failed one. For an RFID project, this is especially true because its usage is relatively new in areas such as supply chain. In this situation, selection of vendors with the appropriate expertise and staying power in the RFID field is critical. These vendors play a major role in helping you design, implement, and manage solutions with only a small set of industry-wide references, best practices, and case studies as aids. They must rely heavily on their own skills, expertise, and resources. They must also possess creative and intuitive skills to help overcome those issues and problems that may present themselves for the first time.

In this chapter, we provide the following:

- A set of guidelines on what you need to consider in your vendor selection process

- Comparison criteria to help differentiate between various vendors

- A pointer to the latest RFID vendor landscape with detailed and categorized lists of key vendors and their capabilities and offerings

Vendor Selection Approach

In Chapter 5, we outlined the framework needed to embark on an RFID solution implementation and deployment. In the *Build and Deploy* phase of the framework, we presented the need for appropriate vendor selection. In this section, we discuss three major approaches to vendor selection.

Best-of-Breed

The Best-of-Breed approach involves selection of the *best vendor* for each specific portion of an RFID project. For example, you can select the best vendor of tags and readers, select another vendor that is best at installing and testing, and select yet another vendor that is best qualified to do application integration or training within your enterprise. The choice of which vendor is the best often depends on the specific application and industry. For example, a particular vendor may offer the best high frequency (HF) tags and readers for rugged environments in factory floor automation applications. The same vendor may not be the best choice for UHF tags and readers for inventory management applications in a packaged goods warehouse.

The Best-of-Breed approach implies that you are in control and manage all aspects of the project in-house.

Top Three Advantages

- Ability to meet the requirements of the project as specified

- Higher chance of a successful project outcome

- More flexibility in substituting another vendor if one does not work out as planned

Top Three Drawbacks

- In-house project management function may drain already scarce resources

- Lack of in-house expertise may lead to inappropriate or incorrect vendor choices

- Integrating multiple vendors' products may escalate the cost of the overall project

One-Stop-Shop

The One-Stop-Shop approach approach requires the selection of one single vendor to act as the *primary contractor* vendor for the RFID project. In this case, the primary contractor often manages the entire lifecycle of the project from design and planning to deployment and maintenance. This usually means that a single vendor is responsible for all phases of the project and takes responsibility for selecting subsequent vendors (sub-contractors) if it cannot fulfill certain aspects of the project on its own. For example, if the primary contractor is a systems integrator, it is likely to rely on an RFID hardware vendor to select the type of tags and readers most suitable for the project.

The One-Stop-Shop approach means one vendor is primarily in control, manages all aspects of the project, and takes responsibility for the overall outcome of the project.

Top Three Advantages

- Single point of contact responsible and accountable for all aspects of the project (a.k.a. one throat to choke)

- More in-house resources available to focus on business-related aspects of the project such as setting up success metrics, return on investment (ROI) analysis, and stakeholder buy-in

- Faster time-to-deployment as project is less dependent on in-house resource and skills constraints

Top Three Drawbacks

- Single point of contact may result in expensive "project restart" in case of a failure

- More complex upgrade/maintenance path due to lack of visibility in details of the project

- Shortfall in required functionality due to inadequate vendor expertise, experience, or focus

Trusted Advisor

The Trusted Advisor approach is a hybrid version of Best-of-Breed and One-Stop-Shop. This approach requires you to maintain the overall project management responsibility in-house and hire a vendor to act as a trusted advisor. This trusted advisor helps you with your vendor selection in an objective manner. In this scenario, a trusted advisor often directly helps with certain aspects of project implementation. For example, if the trusted advisor is a systems vendor, it should be fully capable of architecting the project and deploying both the hardware and software related to the project. For RFID projects in particular, this approach is often the most sensible one. First, due to the fast evolving technological advances, it is much harder for a business implementing an RFID project to keep up with the most recent vendor offerings. A trusted advisor's primary responsibility is to continue to enrich its knowledge base and is more likely to always know the "latest" and the "greatest." Second, a trusted advisor is likely to have a more objective view of other vendors and is not likely to be "tied" to any particular set of vendors.

The Trusted Advisor approach means you are primarily in control and manage most aspects of the project in house. This approach can often maximize the advantages, and minimize the drawbacks of the other two approaches discussed earlier. However, the Trusted Advisor approach may require more out-of-pocket cost than the other two, as you need to spend extra money to hire this trusted advisor. Over the long term, this up-front cost is compensated by a better project outcome—one that provides the most robust design with minimal risk.

Vendor Comparison Criteria

After you have agreed upon the preceding vendor selection approach, you are ready to compare competing vendors. The following criteria will help you make the appropriate choices. Note that we include certain "generic" criteria along with those specific to RFID deployment to make the comparison more meaningful for you.

- **Vital Statistics:** This includes number of employees, recent revenue/profitability figures, geographical reach, and the number of customers. Although these metrics should not be the only determinant, they provide a good health check. In fact, for a fast evolving technology like RFID, small start-up companies with few employees and few customers are nimble and adaptive and are likely to possess the very skills that may not be available at larger, more mainstream companies.

- **The Management Team:** This provides insight into the overall expertise of the vendor. Particularly with smaller vendors, it is important to have a management team that has a solid history of industry experience and expertise, and a demonstrated capability to lead and manage its staff effectively.

- **Customer References:** Although the number and brand name of the references are important, it is more important to determine if these references have deployed projects similar to the ones you are contemplating. The reference should also confirm a track record of high-quality work, on time and within budget.

- **Experience in RFID Technology:** This criterion is important to consider if you believe that RFID experience is critical to the particular phase of the project for which you are considering the vendor. For example, if you are looking at a consulting firm to help your organization implement change management processes, it is more important to find a firm that has experience in change and process management rather than in RFID-specific technology. On the other hand, if you are looking at a vendor to help with a new IT architecture design across your enterprise, it is best to look for a vendor that has adequate RFID architecture design experience, rather than a vendor with a solid history of IT architecture design but only small amount of RFID design experience.

- **Experience in Your Industry:** This criterion is important regardless of the particular phase of the project for which you are considering the vendor. You want to make sure that the vendor has adequate experience and expertise in *your* particular industry. Without this experience, a vendor is not likely to do a good job that requires taking a holistic approach to implementing a solution.

- **Intellectual Property Rights:** Because of the great amount of innovation going on around RFID technology, it is likely that either you or the vendor will end up creating new intellectual property (IP) to implement your solution. The willingness to share your IP with the vendor will open up a new leverage point for you. For example, a consulting firm may be willing to reduce its fee in exchange for the capability to retain non-exclusive rights in the IP it creates for you. Conversely, you may be able to negotiate more attractive licensing terms with a software vendor if you agree to share the IP your engineers may co-create (for example, a connector you build to connect your commercial warehouse management application to the vendor's middleware). Note that this has the side effect of potentially arming your competitors with your IP because the vendor is free to reuse or resell it.

- **Partnerships and Alliances:** A vendor's ecosystem of partners and alliances speaks to its track record, experience, and credibility in the industry. This is particularly true with smaller vendors. Always look for vendors that have a well-known set of partners and alliances that are willing to be used as references. At the same time, a large vendor may also need the backing of small, niche industry-credible vendors that can help fill any gaps the large vendor may have in its offerings.

- **Adherence to Standards:** It is important to assess the importance and impact of standards for your project. For example, if you are a Wal-Mart supplier and have to comply with the EPC standards, you need to make sure that the tag vendor offers compliant and tested EPC tags.

- **Open Architecture:** Products that offer an open architecture can save you from vendor lock-in and ease the integration efforts. This is necessary for any medium- and large-scale RFID project.

Vendor Categories

Now that you have been armed with your selection criteria, you need a basic segmentation of the primary vendor categories to help you with your final selection. Note that many vendors offer solutions that fall into several of these categories.

Tag and Reader Vendors

There is a variety of RFID tag and reader vendors in the market today. Many of these vendors have been in this business for several years, and some for a couple of decades. Whether they are large or small, they often have a successful record of accomplishment in the areas where RFID technology has been applied for quite some time—for example, livestock tracking, toll collection, access control, and factory floor automation. Many offer specialties in specific industries such as livestock. With the opportunity of applying RFID in the supply chain, many new tag and reader vendors have entered the market in the past few years. These vendors generally support EPCglobal standards and offer UHF tags and readers. Some of the older vendors have also started offering EPC-based products. Although many vendors in this category offer both tags and readers, some specialize in building tags or readers only, often for very specific markets such as rugged tags for automobile assembly applications.

RFID Middleware Vendors

RFID middleware is generally most applicable for supply chain applications of RFID. Therefore, RFID middleware products and vendors have been around for only a few years. Prior to the entry of RFID middleware products, most functions performed by today's middleware were customized to fit the specific needs of RFID applications. Because these applications were typically simpler to implement (compared to supply chain applications), many of the sophisticated features of today's RFID middleware were not necessary.

RFID middleware vendors generally fall into two categories: pure play and hybrid. The pure play vendors offer RFID middleware only (see Chapter 3, "Components of RFID Systems," for details about RFID middleware). The hybrid vendors have been offering enterprise IT middleware and have recently entered the RFID middleware space.

Computer Systems Vendors

Computer systems vendors (also known as platform vendors) consist of those that offer computer hardware and/or operating system/platform software for the enterprise. They are a critical category of vendors to evaluate for all RFID projects. After all, any RFID application needs a host computer system or network with which to interact. Additionally, many systems vendors also offer enterprise IT middleware, which is often considered an integral part of the computer systems components. As discussed earlier, many enterprise IT middleware vendors have entered the RFID-specific middleware space and are successfully competing with pure play vendors. As such, some systems vendors are now offering RFID middleware as well. Because of the depth and breadth of their experience and expertise, systems vendors are also excellent candidates for the Trusted Advisor role we discussed earlier.

Application Vendors

Certain application vendors play a critical role in RFID projects, in particular in the supply chain management applications of RFID. These vendors offer an array of software applications that control various aspects of enterprise resource planning (ERP) or supply chain management (SCM) such as inventory control, warehouse management, supply chain execution, and logistics management. RFID tag data is one source of data input to these applications. Therefore, many of the vendors are creating interfaces that allow the flow of RFID data into their software applications in a seamless manner. Depending on the nature of the RFID application (usually for small-scale and isolated deployments), the offerings from these vendors can eliminate or reduce the need for certain RFID middleware features and functionalities.

Systems Integration Vendors

Systems Integration vendors come in two major varieties: large and small. Large systems integrators are well known in the industry and lead the way in designing, implementing, and integrating large-scale enterprise IT applications. Many have started specific RFID practices, often in targeted industries. The majority of RFID projects big enough for large systems integrators are in the supply chain management area. Smaller systems integrators make up the rest of the landscape. Note that many of the vendor types we described earlier also offer systems integration services. We also note a finer distinction between the bigger small integrators, with hundreds of employees, and the "boutique" integrators/consultants with targeted specialties and only dozens of employees.

The choice of the appropriate systems integration vendor should be guided by the applicable criteria we discussed in the previous section. Although large systems integrators can be more expensive, the smaller ones may not always have the resources to implement large-scale RFID solutions.

Value Added Vendors

These vendors are commonly called value added resellers or VARs. VARs essentially act as a selling channel (often local or regional) for the different hardware and software vendors we described earlier. VARs add unique value to the products they resell by creating custom packaging of the original products and by providing other complimentary services such as consulting, installation, training, and integration.

Specialty Services Vendors

These vendors provide the following critical services required for various types of RFID project implementations:

- **Business Consulting:** This is an important but often overlooked service—particularly with brand new RFID implementations that require process reengineering and change management. Many systems integrators, large and small, offer business consulting services. However, certain boutique integrators that target very specific markets and applications can bring significant expertise to the table.

- **Training and Certification:** Another overlooked but important service is RFID training and certification services. Many systems integrators as well as some of the other vendor types discussed in the previous sections offer these services.

- **Managed Services:** Managed services vendors provide outsourcing options for IT infrastructure. In the case of RFID projects, certain enterprises may find it more beneficial to outsource various aspects of their RFID infrastructure to appropriate managed services providers.

- **Market Analysis:** Analyst services are critical, especially because RFID continues to evolve in such a rapid fashion. Analysts provide up-to-date market research, forecasts, vendor comparisons, and surveys that help fine-tune RFID project plans to keep up with a very fast moving target.

- **Third-Party Logistics (3PL):** 3PL providers are unique to the supply chain industry and provide outsourcing services to help manage the logistics associated with supply chain processes. The RFID labeling process at a small- or medium-sized consumer packaged goods manufacturer may benefit from being outsourced completely to a 3PL provider who receives cases and pallets, applies RFID tags on them, and ships them directly to a retail distribution center.

Vendor Guide

Due to the accelerated rate of change in the RFID industry, the vendor landscape is growing and evolving rapidly, and vendor data is changing frequently. Providing a vendor guide here will no doubt be outdated by the time you read it. Instead we provide an extensive and regularly updated RFID vendor guide at this book's companion Web site, *www.rfidfieldguide.com*.

Summary

This chapter concludes the explanations of the framework we laid out in Chapter 5. As noted, vendor selection is critical to the success of an RFID project. Based on your business environment such as resources, skill sets, and funding, you can determine the best vendor selection approach: Best-of-Breed, One-Stop-Shop or Trusted

Advisor. It is equally important to compare different vendors using multiple criteria such as experience in RFID and your industry, and quality of customer references. Some vendors specialize in offering products such as tags and readers. Others may offer multiple products. Some may be pure play vendors—for example, RFID middleware vendors—whereas others might view RFID as an extension of their existing offerings. The vendor lists at *www.rfidfieldguide.com* provide a good starting point to help you select the right vendors for your project.

PART III

THE PATH AHEAD

9

MANDATES AS BUSINESS CATALYSTS

Five Questions This Chapter Will Answer

- What is the role of mandates in business advancement?
- What is the Wal-Mart mandate and how can I comply with it?
- What is the U.S. DoD mandate and how can I comply with it?
- What are some of the other key retail mandates from around the globe?
- What does the U.S. Food and Drug Administration (FDA) say about RFID adoption in the pharmaceutical industry?

A *mandate* is a broad-reaching initiative that catalyzes and, on occasion, jump-starts an entire industry. A mandate finds its inception within the business world or from a government agency and is driven by motives ranging from economics and profitability to services, safety, or even legislative requirements. Mandates can unite consumers and vendors toward a common goal. In many instances, that results in rapid technological advancement and the adoption of strategic policies and standards. For example, barcoding technology gained wide acceptance after Wal-Mart issued a commercial mandate requiring its suppliers to use barcode systems in labeling all their products during the 1980s. Soon after Wal-Mart and its suppliers proved the value of barcoding, it was widely adopted as a worldwide standard method for labeling. This type of mandate is the subject of this chapter. Here, we will focus solely on commercial mandates that have influenced the emergence of RFID technology and catapulted it to the forefront of supply chain and asset management. Note that some of the commercial mandates may be issued by government agencies such as the Department of Defense (DoD), but for commercial reasons as opposed to legislative.

Several mandates have accelerated the use of RFID technology. In 2003, the world's largest military organization, the United States Department of Defense (DoD), and the largest retailer, Wal-Mart, instituted mandates for the adoption of RFID in various applications. They called for their suppliers to adopt RFID in order to continue doing business with them. Several other retailers, including Albertsons, Metro, and Target, require the same of their suppliers. In this chapter, we look at the following:

- Focus on the mandates issued by the DoD and Wal-Mart, evaluating and analyzing their impact on suppliers

- Provide recommendations for the DoD and Wal-Mart suppliers

- Outline RFID adoption guidelines issued by other organizations such as the U.S. Federal Drug Administration and several retailers

As discussed in previous chapters, those suppliers who leverage the work done to meet mandates to also improve the efficiency of their own operations will benefit the most from their efforts.

Wal-Mart and RFID

Background

Wal-Mart uses information technology (IT) as a tool to improve its operations and gain competitive advantage. Several years ago, following an aggressive expansion plan, internal supply chain improvements, and impressive revenue growth, Wal-Mart looked to RFID technology to further improve its operations. Further advances through RFID, such as reduced labor costs, improved inventory control, and advanced market intelligence, appeared to hold significant promise for Wal-Mart. The promise of total supply chain visibility offered by RFID technology was an appealing value proposition. This is because, in spite of billions of dollars of existing investments in supply chain operations, Wal-Mart (and other retailers) experienced problems with lost or misplaced palletized goods. Pallets were sent to the wrong destination or contained fewer cases than originally ordered. Studies show that, on average, products are out of stock in grocery and mass merchandise stores 7% of the time. Some of the most popular items are not available 17% of the time. As a result, retail locations often choose between ordering more than they really need or contend with insufficient stock for the most popular (and often most profitable) items, resulting in lost sales.

Retailers and suppliers are continually seeking new methods for correcting any negative impact to their profit margins. As Wal-Mart perceived it, the more accurate and less labor-intensive tracking enabled by RFID provided the retailer with the expanded supply chain visibility it so critically needed. Because line-of-sight contact is not required to read an RFID tag, Wal-Mart would be much more effective in tracking items in its stores, warehouses, and in transit. This enhanced tracking capability would offer Wal-Mart dramatic improvements over barcode methods, which required much more labor-intensive and time-consuming methods of handling and scanning goods.

RFID would allow Wal-Mart to track individual pallets, cases, or even single items. For example, when a Wal-Mart store received a pallet containing cereal boxes, the store manager could quickly discern precisely how many cases and individual cereal boxes had arrived. This information could be derived not only from a tag on the pallet, but also from individual, differentiating tags on every case and box. By integrating this data with the store's existing warehouse management system, that manager would know immediately when the supply was low so that a new order could be placed. With barcodes, such item-level verification of goods is impractical, because of the vast amount of handling required to open up every case in a pallet and scan its contents at the receiving dock. With RFID, the entire contents of a pallet, even those containing a variety of different products, could be identified easily and efficiently with minimal handling.

Having selected RFID technology, Wal-Mart's executives embarked on the same path that they had followed two decades before, when they mandated the use of UPC barcodes, ushering in their widespread use throughout the industry. This time, they developed a similar mandate to usher in the era of widespread use of RFID. Looking at the complexity of this operation, however, Wal-Mart modified its mandate to only case- and pallet-level tagging. Tagging of individual items may happen at a future date.

Wal-Mart Mandate

On June 11, 2003, Linda Dillman, the CIO of Wal-Mart, revealed that its top 100 suppliers would be required to put RFID tags carrying Electronic Product Codes (EPC) on pallets and cases by January 1, 2005. This was a global directive, and Dillman announced that the company would begin a pilot by the end of 2003. Subsequently, Wal-Mart's distribution center near Dallas, Texas, was selected as the site for the pilot. The company organized a conference for its suppliers in November 2003 in Bentonville, Arkansas, to provide further clarification on the mandate, including specifications for the tags to be used.

Among the key points of the Wal-Mart mandate were the following requirements:

- One hundred percent of all cases and pallets sent by the top 100 suppliers into the Texas Distribution Center were to be tagged by January 1, 2005. After several pilots in 2004, the target was reset to 65%, on average, as an achievable target due to trouble reading tags on metal and liquid.

- Eight stores in the Dallas/Fort Worth area would participate in the initial rollout, with subsequent rollouts beyond that area.

- All suppliers were to tag cases and pallets by end of 2006.

- Ultra High Frequency (UHF) tags would be used.

- Per the current EPCglobal standards, Class 0 and Class 1 tags were to be used initially, with a shift to EPC Generation 2 tags (that is, next generation tags) after that standard is properly defined (see Chapter 4, "Standards Related to RFID," for details). (Note that Gen 2 standard was ratified in December 2004. Wal-Mart is not likely to force the transition to Gen 2 tags until they are widely available.)

- Data would be communicated to and from Wal-Mart via RetailLink and Electronic Data Interchange (EDI), with no use of the EPCglobal Network because the standard was still under development (see Chapter 3, "Components of RFID Systems," and Chapter 4, "Standards Related to RFID," for details on the EPCglobal Network).

- The EPC tag with embedded Global Trade Inventory Number (GTIN) and serial number was to be used, and the EPC number would be GTIN based.

- A mandatory 100% read accuracy was specified for tagged goods within 10 feet of the reader.

- Cases containing one item (for example, a couch or a TV set) must be tagged.

- A separate pharmaceutical tagging project would also get underway with specific requirements for handling prescription drugs.

Wal-Mart announced in the spring of 2004 that several vendors had begun shipping their goods to the retailer with RFID tags, commencing the first real-world test of the mandate. The company planned to use a phased approach in requiring all of its more than 25,000 suppliers to follow this mandate. This is illustrated in the following timeline in Figure 9.1.

Phased approach for 25,000+ suppliers

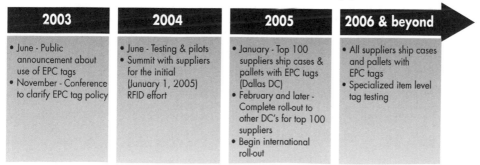

2003	2004	2005	2006 & beyond
• June - Public announcement about use of EPC tags • November - Conference to clarify EPC tag policy	• June - Testing & pilots • Summit with suppliers for the initial (January 1, 2005) RFID effort	• January - Top 100 suppliers ship cases & pallets with EPC tags (Dallas DC) • February and later - Complete roll-out to other DC's for top 100 suppliers • Begin international roll-out	• All suppliers ship cases and pallets with EPC tags • Specialized item level tag testing

FIGURE 9.1   Milestones for the Wal-Mart RFID Mandate

Implications for Suppliers

The implications of this mandate for Wal-Mart's suppliers are enormous. Although the first phase of the mandate focuses primarily on the top 100 suppliers, it corresponds to the use of EPC tags on approximately one billion cases per year (approximately one-eighth of Wal-Mart's annual total). In addition, Wal-Mart wants to achieve that goal in just over 12 months. Because EPC standards are still in the developmental stages, this rapid transition has the potential for continued change, and for some suppliers, a wasted investment in technology infrastructure that may become obsolete as standards evolve.

However, several factors can offset the potential downside hazards for suppliers. Wal-Mart is fully aware that it can derive the greatest benefit from its mandate only if the vast majority of its suppliers successfully adopt RFID technology. Therefore, the company also has been working closely with EPCglobal to develop and deploy the most feasible set of standards. The retailer also has expressed a concern about consumer privacy to the EPC working groups, so that effective policies about privacy will be carefully considered (see Chapter 10, "Security and Privacy," for more on this subject). In addition, Wal-Mart has stated its intent to work with suppliers to resolve the difficulties in tagging items containing metal or liquid, which is still a technical challenge (see Chapter 3 for details on why this is the case). One example of Wal-Mart's flexibility: resetting the goal requiring its top 100 suppliers to tag 100% of cases and pallets by January 1, 2005. Now, Wal-Mart expects approximately 65% of cases and pallets to be tagged, based on trials in 2004.

Wal-Mart is also working to ease suppliers' concerns over costs of RFID technology implementation by keeping the standards open and non-proprietary. Because several other retailers have announced plans to adopt EPC tags, suppliers providing goods to other retailers such as Target and Albertsons can leverage their initial, Wal-Mart related, investments across the larger customer base. In a show of support for standards, both Linda Dillman (CIO of Wal-Mart) and Paul Singer (CIO of Target) shared the stage at a retail conference in May of 2004 and announced their support for the EPC standards. This type of major support should result in similar announcements from other retailers, thus reducing the risk that suppliers might face by investing in disparate technologies to meet individual customers' requirements. The resulting volumes should also drive down the prices of tags and readers.

Implications for RFID Component Vendors

In an emerging area such as EPC, vendors can improve their competitive positioning by paying special attention to standards and the resulting implications for architecture. RFID component vendors also must focus on evaluating specific problems faced by their customers and then designing solutions. For example, the area of data collection and synchronization is likely to be a serious concern. Item-level tagging could increase the number of tags so dramatically that the computing infrastructure could become heavily taxed. Can you imagine the number of tags required and the amount of data generated if the United States Postal Service started using RFID to improve its operations and putting an RFID tag on every piece of mail delivered? That would require tens of billions of tags annually and generate many Terabytes of data. Those vendors that have built their solutions for such large-scale volume will be able to compete successfully. Vendors that adhere to open standards such as Java, XML, and EPCglobal are likely to be at an advantage over their competition as companies in open loop supply chains seek to exchange data among their peers (that is, engage in data synchronization).

Vendors looking to succeed on all levels will have to take the initiative by educating their customers about the benefits of RFID. Vendor expertise with regard to business processes and turnkey solutions, based on well-defined frameworks, will help ease customer sales and marketing cycle.

U.S. Department of Defense and RFID

Background

At the same time Wal-Mart was developing its mandate requiring its suppliers to implement EPC tags, the U.S. Department of Defense (DoD) was devising its own mandate for asset management. With more than 100,000 ground combat and tactical vehicles, over 250,000 wheeled vehicles, more than 1,000 strategic missiles, over 300 ships, more than 15,000 aircraft and helicopters, and numerous other supplies for the troops, the DoD's inventory has been valued at more than $700 billion. At any given time, a significant part of this inventory is in transit, sometimes in hostile areas, making inventory management extraordinarily challenging. Effective management of this inventory is critical both from financial and national security points of view.

A report by the General Accounting Office (GAO) revealed that overall, the DoD lacked complete and reliable information about its assets. Therefore, its capability to evaluate the condition of its inventory or adequately compare the reported inventory to the actual physical inventory was sub-optimal.

To address this situation, the DoD evaluated a variety of Automatic Identification Technologies (AIT). First, it benchmarked selected companies in the retail, wholesale, and transportation industries to determine how they managed their supply chain and inventories effectively. The DoD then sought out selected industrial experts to analyze various barcode standards and their enabling technologies. Following these studies, the DoD decided to use commercial standards and off-the-shelf technologies for the automatic identification of objects. Key to this decision was its plan to identify separate items through a Unique ID (UID) method for each part. On July 2, 2003, the DoD issued an official policy, mandating UID as a requirement for all applicable solicitations issued on or after January 1, 2004 (see "What is UID?" for details).

What is UID?

A Unique IDentifier (UID) is a set of data for tangible assets that is globally unique and unambiguous, ensures data integrity, and supports multiple applications. The DoD Instruction 5000.64 requires that accountable records be established for all property having a unit acquisition cost of $5,000 or more as well as items that are classified or sensitive. UID provides a mechanism to address this requirement. Unique identification of a tangible item involves two key considerations. First, the enterprise that created the item is uniquely identified by its enterprise identifier (for example, Uniform Code Council (UCC)/EAN Company Prefix, ANSI T1.220 Number). Second, the item within a given enterprise is uniquely identified. There are different ways to devise these unique serial numbers. By combining the two identifiers, a single unique number (UID) for each item can be created. Further details on the topic can be found in the "Department of Defense Guide to Uniquely Identifying Tangible Items" and at *www.uidsupport.com.*

RFID technology appeared to be an excellent way to implement UID. The department already had experience using RFID technology, having used the active tag-based system since the early 1990s. The developers involved viewed it as a technology with the potential to improve inventory management and asset visibility through item-level tracking throughout the supply chain—at home or in the field. That system proved remarkably effective during the second Gulf War in 2003 (see the case study Operation Enduring Freedom / Operation Iraqi Freedom in Appendix A for details). Use of RFID as a tool to implement UID had another advantage. Now, the DoD suppliers would not need two different identification numbers for products that were going to consumers as well as to the DoD. For example, a computer manufacturer whose computers are used in a commercial enterprise as well as in an aircraft carrier does not have to maintain two numbering schemes, one for each market. An EPC for each computer is all that the manufacturer has to track.

Details of the Mandate

On October 2, 2003, the Office of the Under Secretary of Defense issued its first memorandum outlining the DoD's RFID policy, which was followed with an update on February 20, 2004 and the final update on July 30, 2004. Following the DoD's success in leveraging active systems for identification purposes, the policy directed the continuance of active tags currently in use. It also required suppliers to use passive EPC tags on those cases, pallets, and individual items requiring a UID that were solicited after October 1, 2004, for delivery of material on or after January 1, 2005. The deadline was later revised to early 2005. In accordance with this policy, the DoD distribution centers in Susquehanna, Pennsylvania and San Joaquin, California would deploy the necessary infrastructure to read these tags by the due date. The memorandum also provides details about business guidelines for the use of information collected through RFID. As with Wal-Mart, the department planned to engage in phased roll-outs with clearly defined milestones. This is illustrated in the following timeline in Figure 9.2.

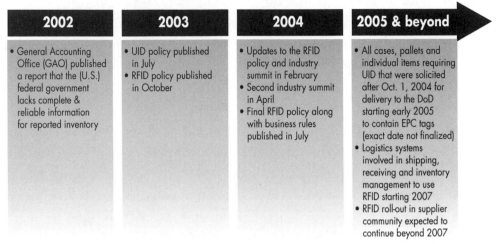

FIGURE 9.2   Milestones for the DoD RFID Mandate

Through this policy, the DoD intended to improve item management and business functions by doing the following:

- Providing near real-time visibility for all classes of supplies and materials in transit

- Providing content-level details (including boxed items) for all classes of supplies and materials in transit

- Providing reliable mechanisms for non-intrusive identification and data collection to enable enhanced inventory management

- Providing enhanced item-level visibility for various DoD operations

The DoD published a draft of its business rules that maps the preceding policy points to specific tagging requirements by layers of logistics units (that is, cases, pallets, and containers). This is illustrated in Table 9.1.

Note:

The DoD prefers EPC UHF Generation 2 tags (gen 2 tags), but will accept current EPC Class 0 and Class 1 UHF tags until Generation 2 tags become available on a wide-scale basis. (Note that Gen 2 standard was ratified in December 2004, so it will take some time before Gen 2 tags are widely available.)

TABLE 9.1   Details of the DoD's RFID Mandate by Item Type[1]

RFID Layer	Item Type	Tag Type	Class Tag	Frequency	Read Range	Requirement
0	Individual Item (e.g. lose items)	Passive	0, 1 or higher	UHF	3 m	Not yet Required
1	Item Package	Passive	0, 1 or higher	UHF	3 m	Required on UID/specified items from Jan 1, 2005°
2	Transport Unit, Case	Passive	0, 1 or higher	UHF	3 m	Required Jan 1, 2005°
3	Unit Load, Pallet	Passive	0, 1 or higher	UHF	3 m	Required Jan 1, 2005°
4	Freight Container, Palletized Unit Move Shipment	Active tag w/content level details	N/A	N/A	> 3 m	Operational now– selectively

The Read Range in Table 9.1 is specified in meters per DoD policy. Three meters is approx. 10 feet.

° Deadline later revised to early 2005.

The DoD also mandated that beginning in 2007 and beyond, its logistics systems involved in shipping, receiving, and inventory management will use RFID to perform business transactions; funding for such systems will hinge on compliance with this policy. Further details about the DoD policy can be found at *www.acq.osd.mil/log/rfid*.

Implications for Suppliers

As with the Wal-Mart mandate, the implications and challenges of the DoD mandate are enormous for its suppliers, which number more than 43,000. The DoD has now decided to use an EPC tag data numbering scheme as well as DoD tag data constructs for encoding. Because the DoD mandate is not limited to its top suppliers, smaller firms will be particularly challenged with the pressure to comply. The DoD's requirement for item-level tagging on certain items will force suppliers to establish more complex RFID tagging operations in the near term.

[1] Radio Frequency Identification (RFID) Policy, The Under Secretary of Defense, Oct 2, 2003, and Radio Frequency Identification Policy (RFID)—UPDATE, The Under Secretary of Defense, Feb 20, 2004.

Several positive factors do exist that may compensate for the negatives:

- Like Wal-Mart, the DoD wants its RFID policy and UID initiative to succeed, so that the department can achieve its goal of total asset visibility and efficient inventory management. To that end, the agency has been working with industry leaders. For example, it has established a Vendor Advisory Group (VAG) to help define technical specifications and standards as well as policies and procedures. Since last year, the department has held several industry summits to educate and solicit feedback from suppliers and vendors.

- The DoD has finalized its data-encoding scheme and published it together with the final version of the business guidelines and rules to provide guidance to suppliers.

- The DoD's interest in and support of EPC and ISO standards for RFID deployment will help to achieve consensus between the two standards organizations, thereby benefiting industry as a whole.

- The DoD is applying a phased approach to RFID compliance, based on a timeline with specific milestones. In that scheme, new solicitations or renewals after October 1, 2004, for delivery beginning on January 1, 2005, will require compliance by January 1, 2005. However, two points are worth noting here. First, suppliers that have on-going contracts or those who are involved in new solicitations before the cut-off date will have some leniency beyond the initial date. Second, the DoD has revised the deadline to sometime in early 2005, citing a delay in publishing guidelines to suppliers. The DoD expects roll-outs to continue beyond 2007.

The department has deployed the use of RFID technology in several places to acquire operational experience. The DoD has conducted two pilots, one for the shipment of Meals Ready to Eat (MRE) and the second for the shipment of chemical protection suits. Both active and passive tags were used in these pilots. Although the DoD accepted the results as generally positive, these test programs did reveal that some processes needed to be reengineered for RFID. For example, those processes where other items generating RF noise in proximity of the test area caused interference with RFID systems and affected performance.

Recommendations for Suppliers of Wal-Mart, Other Retailers, and the DoD

To enable suppliers to comply with Wal-Mart, DoD, and other retailers' mandates for RFID technology, the following steps are recommended:

- **Agree to comply and participate in the process.** Both Wal-Mart and the DoD are fully engaged in the process of integrating RFID technology into their operations. Other retailers are also supporting the use of RFID. It is critical to work with the retailers and organizations such as the DoD rather than opt out of the process. Begin an approach that allows you to stay aware of policy updates and become compliant (see Chapter 5, "Framework for Deployment," for details on how to determine rationale for RFID deployment and effectively deploy it in an enterprise).

- **Implement a compliance program after careful study and planning.** Although compliance is inevitable, planning is essential. As RFID technology continues to mature, seek vendors who provide flexible and proven solutions that can be upgraded (for example, readers that can be upgraded (preferably via firmware) from detecting Class 0 or Class 1 tags to Generation 2 tags, systems that are robust enough to increase tag detection capacity of the reader to accommodate item-level tagging). A phased approach to compliance makes the most sense. For that reason, a pilot is recommended, with the lessons learned during that pilot then applied. For Wal-Mart suppliers, use the lessons from their pilot program for full-scale compliance for all the SKUs under consideration. For DoD suppliers, it is critical to take special steps if you supply an item that requires a UID.

- **Take a holistic approach to solving this problem.** Merely "slapping" tags on the cases that go to Wal-Mart or the DoD (a method known as *slap & ship*) may introduce pitfalls, increase your costs, and minimize potential benefits. Instead, take a look at your business processes to see how the added information and tracking provided by EPC tags can be used to make better decisions about streamlining your own operations, understand and respond to customers, and improve your own supply chain. In some cases, you may not have a choice but to implement slap & ship in the short term to address an impending mandate. Even in those cases, it is important to plan how your operations need to be modified to accommodate the addition of tags. It may not be sufficient to simply put tags on the cases. Tags need to be tested by using readers in various plants and warehouses. Workers, from the shop floor mechanic to the IT systems administrator, will need training on the handling of this technology. Focus on your unique business case and establish priorities for the pilot program. Watch out for obvious tracking limitations of the UHF tags when applied to metal or liquid. If your product falls in this category, talk to Wal-Mart, the DoD, or other appropriate retailers for exceptions. (Wal-Mart has accepted this current limitation for UHF-based tags and reset its expectations.) They may even share their knowledge on this topic, derived from others in your situation.

- **Select vendors carefully.** Select consultants or system integrators that have experience in your industry, so that they can design an RFID solution that is right for your own needs. The vendor criteria in Chapter 8 and the vendor guide at *www.rfidfieldguide.com* (the companion Web site to this book) provide a good starting point to find these vendors. In the same way, select software packages that exhibit flexible and standards-based architecture, such as XML, thus enabling you to leverage that software as RFID technology becomes more sophisticated and complex. If you are a supplier for the DoD, such scalability is particularly important, given the DoD's goal of uniting ISO and EPC standards for RFID. To further protect yourself, ask vendors for assurance related to functional compliance with the mandate(s).

- **Align with Wal-Mart's plans for the roll-out if you are a Wal-Mart supplier.** You may benefit in saving time and money, and increase your chances of success during the initial pilot phase and again in full-scale deployment.

- **Educate end-user customers.** Create a plan that will educate end-user customers about EPC tags, especially if you are planning to do any item-level tagging.

RFID Initiatives at Other Organizations

Apart from the Wal-Mart and DoD mandates, several other large retailers and institutions have published RFID compliance guidelines for their suppliers. Some are similar to Wal-Mart's standards. Others such as the U.S. FDA (Food and Drug Administration) are different, illustrating the breadth and applicability of RFID. These guidelines are summarized in Table 9.2.

TABLE 9.2 RFID Adoption Plans and Supplier Guidelines for Selected Major Organizations

Organization	RFID Adoption Plan	Tag Type	Status
Albertsons	• Top 100 suppliers to tag cases and pallets by April 2005	UHF tags based on EPC	• Pilot in process
(U.S.) Food and Drug Administration (FDA) *Note: Not a mandate but a roadmap that could turn into a mandate*	• Unique identification (mass serialization) of some drugs most likely to be counterfeited, at pallet, case, and package level by Dec 2005 • Unique identification (mass serialization) of most drugs, at pallet and case level by Dec 2006 • Unique identification (mass serialization) of all drugs at pallet and case level, and most drugs at package level, by Dec 2007 • Acquisition and use of RFID technology by all manufacturers, wholesalers, chain drug stores, hospitals and most small retailers by Dec 2007	Passive	• Various suppliers and others working on plans to comply • FDA issued a pharmaceutical tagging initiative in Nov 2004, accelerating RFID pilots in this industry • Subsequently, several pharmaceutical companies announced initiatives to tag individual bottles of prescription medicine
Metro Group (Germany)	• Top 100 suppliers to send RFID tagged pallets to 10 distribution centers and 50 stores by Nov 2004 • Plans to use RFID throughout its supply chain—in store as well as with partners. RFID deployment in 800 stores by 2007	UHF tags based on EPC, some early work based on HF tags	• Working on pilots with partners and in-store • Opened an RFID-enabled future store in Summer 2004
Target	• Top suppliers to apply RFID tags on pallets and cases sent to select regional distribution centers by late spring 2005	UHF tags based on EPC	• All suppliers in compliance by 2007 • Working on pilots

TABLE 9.2   continued

Organization	RFID Adoption Plan	Tag Type	Status
Tesco (UK)	• Suppliers to tag pallets and cases starting Sept 2004 • All suppliers likely on-board by 2007. End date not confirmed	UHF tags based on EPC	• Tracking non-food items between its distribution center and several stores • DVD tracking pilot in select locations

Summary

Several mandates for RFID usage, notably from Wal-Mart and the DoD, have created critical momentum in the market for the use and adoption of RFID technology. In general, these mandates adhere to EPC standards, however they leave out parts of the EPCglobal Network (such as the global registry) that are under development. The partial adherence to standards as well as the developing nature of the technology is likely to make RFID adoption somewhat complex for the suppliers. However, staying out on the sideline is not an option. If you are a supplier to these entities, you are likely to benefit more by complying with these mandates. Because RFID deployments take time and vary based on the environmental conditions (for example, RF noise in warehouses), you should start pilots as soon as possible to gain experience. In fact, to get the most benefit from the deployment, you should create plans to deploy RFID in other parts of your internal or external organizations—for example, your supply chain. The information provided in earlier chapters—deployment frameworks, organizational considerations, cost-benefit analysis, and the vendor landscape—should help you carry out these deployment plans.

10

SECURITY AND PRIVACY

Five Questions This Chapter Will Answer

- How do security and privacy relate to one another?
- What kind of security issues should be considered when designing an RFID application?
- How do tags and readers prevent unauthorized access to RFID data?
- How can the protection of confidential or personal data in RFID systems be ensured?
- Why is it important to educate consumers about RFID?

In the pre-Internet world, data was either kept on paper, on stand-alone computers, or on private computer networks not easily accessible to hackers and intruders. Since the mid 1990s, the widespread use of the Internet has created large amounts of data that is exposed on what is essentially a public network. The dramatic increase in the amount of easily accessible data in our everyday lives brings with it a set of new security and privacy concerns. For example, part of the Internet's popularity centers on electronic commerce, or *e-commerce*. The Internet offers a convenient way to shop and perform a variety of financial transactions. However, this also means that consumers could reveal confidential or private data, such as detailed identity and financial information over a conceivably insecure medium to potentially untrustworthy parties. A common example of this kind of disclosure occurs each time someone applies for a loan, mortgage, or just opens a bank account online. To help keep data secure, technology solutions, such as encryption, identity management, firewalls, and intrusion detection, are routinely employed.

In many ways, the issues of security and privacy related to the use of RFID applications mirror those created with the introduction of the Internet. RFID tags are essentially tiny little computers that hold information that can be confidential and personal, and potentially available on a public network. RFID applications identify ordinary objects and access or transmit data about those objects, or the object holders (for example, consumers), by radio frequency through the air around us. If left unprotected, this data becomes exposed to malicious or unauthorized use and distribution. As RFID technology and its applications become ubiquitous, nearly every item imaginable—a car tire, a box of cereal, a door handle, or a beloved pet—will carry an RFID tag whose data could be compromised. Consumer privacy groups contend that RFID tag data could conceivably be used by commercial or governmental agencies to track and trace people's actions and belongings in ways that might violate individual rights to privacy.

Using the Internet as our blueprint, in this chapter we provide the following:

- An overview of existing and potential security and privacy issues related to RFID

- Practical solutions, guidelines, and best practices for navigating these issues

Distinguishing Between Security and Privacy Issues

Although the terms *security* and *privacy* are often used interchangeably, it is important to understand the distinction between the two as illustrated in Figure 10.1. This will help you devise an effective plan to address the issues surrounding security and privacy in your application.

Security concerns revolve around vulnerabilities and solutions for *protecting confidential data* from *unauthorized* access and manipulation. Data about people, corporations, and objects that has been deemed confidential should be subject to protection and safekeeping. Deliberate security breaches involve the theft and use of such data by a third party for profit, mischief, or malice. Although privacy violations can happen because of security breaches, our focus in this chapter on privacy is as described next.

Our focus here on privacy issues is about the potential *misuse of data* by *authorized* users which leads to violation and invasion of individual or business privacy. In relation to RFID technology, hotly contested topics around privacy do not relate to security, per se. Instead, they primarily relate to the authorized collection of personal data that could potentially be misused or abused by authorities. In the United States, the oft-repeated Orwellian motif, "Big Brother is watching you," reflects concern that the same entities responsible for collecting and managing data about a population—for providing valuable services to it—may be using that data for activities such as surveillance, monitoring, tracking, and profiling of citizens. This concern applies as well to seemingly less-intrusive acts of "targeted selling" (that is, tracking consumer-spending habits to aim specific advertising at unwitting consumers).

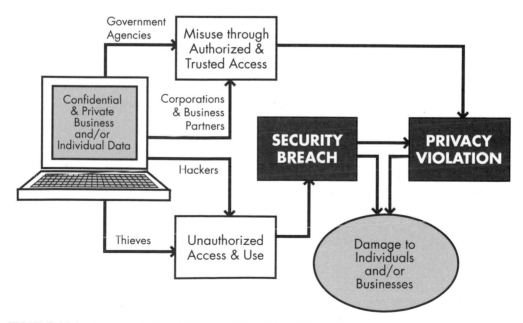

FIGURE 10.1 **Distinguishing Between Privacy and Security**

We note that although *individual* privacy concerns are more often discussed and debated publicly, *business enterprises* are also concerned with breaches of security that result in unauthorized access and possible manipulation of private or confidential corporate data. For example, in a supply chain RFID application where RFID tags are used to track inventory of products, a business partner who accesses confidential inventory data or tracks the movement of inventory by accessing the tag data, with or without authorization, compromises certain corporate data and possibly hampers that corporation's capability to negotiate better prices with its suppliers or customers.

In the next sections, we point to areas of security vulnerabilities, assess risks for enterprises and consumers, and outline a range of possible solutions. We conclude with a discussion of RFID-related privacy issues and offer a set of best practices that help address these issues.

Security Challenges

Security issues that exist in RFID systems are, in many ways, similar to security issues in computer systems and networks. Ultimately, the objective in both types of systems is to secure and protect the stored data and the data communication in and between various parts of the system. However, dealing with security in RFID systems is often more challenging due to two factors. First, the communication method in RFID systems is contactless and wireless, making them susceptible to eavesdropping. Second, the amount of computing power and programmability in RFID systems, especially on the tags, is bounded by the cost requirements of the tags themselves. More precisely, the less expensive the tags need to be in a particular application, the less computing power they will have (that is, the less programmability against security threats can be implemented). We explore these challenges and limitations as we next discuss the major vulnerability points in RFID systems and offer the means to assess the risks of security breaches and suggest appropriate solutions to protect against them.

Areas of Security Vulnerability in RFID Components

In an RFID system, data is vulnerable to unauthorized access while it is stored in the tag, the reader or the host computer, or when it is being transmitted from one of these components to another. We classify the areas of security vulnerability into four categories and describe each separately in the following sections.

Tag Data Access Vulnerability

A tag often contains an integrated circuit (IC), essentially a microchip with memory. Data on the tag can be compromised in similar fashion to data on a computer. Tag data is vulnerable when an unauthorized party either accesses an authorized reader or configures a reader to communicate with a specific tag. In such a scenario, the unauthorized user can access the data on the tag as if he was performing an authorized read. In the case of writeable tags, data might also be modified or even deleted by an unauthorized user.

Tag and Reader Communication Vulnerability

When a tag transmits data to a reader, or a reader interrogates a tag for data, the data travels through the air via radio waves. During this exchange, data is vulnerable. Some methods of exploiting the vulnerability of such wireless exchange include the following:

- **An unauthorized reader hijacks the data.** In this scenario, an unauthorized reader simply intercepts the data transmitted by the tag.

- **A third party jams or spoofs data communication.** An unauthorized party might utilize several methods to prevent communication between the tag and the reader. One common way, spoofing, creates electromagnetic interference by overloading the reader with so many fake tag responses that the reader cannot distinguish any of the legitimate tag responses. This method is also called a *denial-of-service* attack.

- **An imposter tag sends data.** An imposter tag supplies unwanted information or erroneous data to the reader, effectively tricking the RFID system to receive, process, and act on inaccurate tag data.

Vulnerability of Data Inside the Reader

When a tag sends its data to the reader, the reader stores the information in its memory and uses it to perform a number of functions before it purges that data and/or sends it to the host computer system. During these processes, the reader functions just like any other computer where traditional security vulnerabilities and issues exist. Currently, the majority of readers on the market are proprietary, and they may not provide an interface that allows users to enhance the reader's security features beyond the capabilities offered by the vendor. This limitation makes careful selection of a reader especially important.

Vulnerability of the Host Computer System

After data has moved from a tag, through a reader, and onto a host computer, it is subject to the vulnerabilities that already exist at the host level. These vulnerabilities are beyond the scope of this book. Interested readers should refer to appropriate books on computer or network security.

Assessing Security Risks in RFID Applications

The risks of data being compromised during a security breach vary depending on the type of application. For the purposes of discussion in this chapter, we broadly categorize RFID applications into two types, Consumer and Enterprise, and describe the risks for each type in more detail.

Consumer Application Risks

Consumer RFID applications include those that collect or manage data about consumers, or are "touched" by consumers. Typical applications in this category include access control, electronic toll collection, and any application that involves tagging of items in a retail store. With consumer applications, the risk of security breaches can be damaging both to the business entities deploying the system and to the consumer. We discuss the potential damages to businesses in the next section. The damage to the consumer is generally related to violation or invasion of privacy but may also include direct or indirect financial damage.

Even in cases where no personal consumer data is directly collected or maintained by an RFID system, if the consumer touches (handles, holds, or carries) an object with an RFID tag, there is potential to create an association between the consumer and the tag. Such an association conveys personal data about a consumer and may have privacy risks. For example, RFID tags used to control entry into a car do not contain any information about the owner of the car, but there still exists the threat that the holder of the tagged car key could be tracked. This can happen only if it was possible to build a series of sophisticated readers, strategically placed to interrogate the tagged key.

Enterprise Application Risks

Enterprise RFID applications are those internal to a business or a collection of businesses. Typical enterprise applications include any number of supply chain management process enhancing applications (for example, inventory control or logistics management). Another application is in the area of industrial automation where RFID systems are used to track manufacturing processes on the factory floor. Here, the risk of security breaches is generally limited to damaging the enterprise only. These security breaches can disrupt business processes and functions or compromise confidential corporate information.

For example, hackers can disrupt RFID-enabled supply chain processes among business partners through spoofing and mounting denial-of-service attacks. Also, competitors can steal confidential inventory data or gain access to specific industrial automation practices. In other cases, hackers can access and publicize similar confidential enterprise data. This can also compromise a business's competitive advantage. In cases where several enterprises are jointly using an RFID system, for example, to create a more efficient supply chain between suppliers and manufacturers, breach of tag data security is likely to be harmful to all the businesses involved.

Solutions for Securing and Protecting RFID Data

In this section, we discuss some of the more common solutions for securing and protecting RFID data and communication to address the vulnerabilities associated with tag data (*Tag Data Access Vulnerability*) and tag and reader interaction (*Tag and Reader Communication Vulnerability*). Table 10.1 shows a summary of these solutions. Vulnerabilities related to data already inside the reader (*Vulnerability of Data Inside the Reader*) or at the host computer level (*Vulnerability of the Host Computer System*) are beyond the scope of this book[1].

---

[1] As mentioned earlier, the reader functions like a computer when it receives data from a tag for processing. Therefore, this data can and should be secured in a similar manner to securing data on a computer.

TABLE 10.1   Solutions for Securing and Protecting RFID Data

SOLUTION	Vulnerability Addressed	
	Tag data Access	Tag and Reader Communication
Securing Premises	✓	
Using Read Only Tags	✓	
Limiting the Range of Communication		✓
Implementing a Proprietary Protocol	✓	✓
Shielding	✓	✓
Using the Kill Command Feature	✓	
Physically Destroying a Tag	✓	
Authenticating and Encrypting	✓	✓
Selective Blocking	✓	✓

Securing Premises

Using traditional means of securing the premises (with lock and key) where tagged objects are found (for example, in a warehouse or on a factory floor) addresses some vulnerabilities associated with direct tag access. This solution works well *if* all tags are guaranteed to be in certain locations and are not expected to move outside of the four walls of an enterprise. Many RFID applications, however, require tagged objects to move between two or more enterprises and possibly into consumers' hands.

Using Read-Only Tags

Making tags read-only is a "designed-in" security measure that protects tag data from being changed or deleted by an unauthorized reader. However, by itself, this solution leaves data vulnerable to unauthorized reads—especially if tagged objects are easily accessible or public.

Limiting the Range of Communication Between Tag and Reader

Using operating frequencies and/or other physical attributes of the tag, reader, or antenna in order to limit the range of communication between a tag and a reader minimizes the degree of vulnerability. Although this solution effectively limits the potential threat of unauthorized readers accessing tag data, it does not guarantee secured communications at all times.

Implementing a Proprietary Communication Protocol

The strategy of implementing a proprietary protocol is useful for applications where interoperability and data sharing is not a requirement. It involves implementing a communication protocol and data encoding/encryption scheme that is not publicly accessible. Depending on the sophistication of the protocol and the underlying encoding method, this approach can offer a good level of security. However, with the benefits resulting from sharing RFID data (for example, among supply chain partners) and the adoption of wide-ranging RFID standards, proprietary protocols are not always practical. These proprietary protocols will hinder RFID data and application interoperability, which will result in fewer benefits at potentially elevated price points.

Shielding

Also known as the *Faraday Cage* approach, this technique involves enclosing tagged objects in materials such as metal mesh or foil that blocks electromagnetic wave penetration or propagation. Although this method effectively secures RFID tags, when the tag is shielded, RFID readers cannot read the tag either, thereby voiding RFID's benefits. For some RFID applications, temporarily shielding reduces the risk of unauthorized access. For example, the FasTrak electronic toll collection system in California provides users with a Mylar bag to encase their transponders when not driving through toll plazas. Applications that tag money or sensitive documents provide another example because the tagged objects can be placed in foil lined wallets, purses, or briefcases.

Using the Kill Command Feature

The Kill command is designed to disable a tag that is equipped to accept such a command. Upon receipt of the Kill command, the tag ceases to function and cannot receive or transmit data. Both shielding and the Kill command render the tag unreadable. However, shielding is not permanent because it can be removed and a tag can again become functional. On the other hand, a Kill command permanently renders the tag non-functional.

Killing a tag may be warranted in cases where the physical packaging of the tag does not permit shielding. EPCglobal has presented this solution as an effective means of ensuring consumer privacy after retail points of sale. The most significant advantage of this solution is the assurance of consumer privacy. Purchased items and associations to individuals cannot be tracked beyond their point of sale.

The primary disadvantage of this solution concerns limited tag functionality relevant to both consumers and businesses. Consider, for example, a scenario where a consumer returns an undamaged product such as an item of clothing. If the tag had previously been killed at the initial point of sale, the capability to efficiently update inventory, utilize smart shelves, and/or manage a supply chain was also terminated at the issuance of the Kill command.

In a more futuristic scenario, imagine that a milk carton is tagged with a variety of information including its price and expiration date. Imagine also that the refrigerator of the future has a built-in reader to alert the consumer when product expiration is near or has been reached. If the tag were killed at the point of sale, a consumer would not be able to utilize RFID's potential conveniences. In this case, alerting the consumer to use or replace the expiring carton of milk.

Physically Destroying a Tag

Physical destruction of a tag achieves the same results and possesses the same advantages and disadvantages as the Kill command. One added advantage to this solution, however, is that you don't have to wonder if the Kill command actually worked. However, in some applications, it is not always easy or possible to locate and remove a tag—to destroy it—because it may be imperceptible, inaccessible, or embedded.

Authenticating and Encrypting

Various authentication and/or encryption schemes can be used to ensure that only authorized readers can access certain tags and their data. An authentication scheme can be as simple as "locking" tag data until an authorized reader provides a valid password to unlock the data. More sophisticated schemes may include both authentication and encryption of data that provide more layers of protection. Although such schemes are not without their own vulnerabilities, cost is the most prohibitive factor in implementing sophisticated authentication and encryption solutions in RFID systems. If mandates require low-cost tagging for inexpensive items, the tags are likely to have reduced programmability for authentication and encryption. High-value items such as jewelry or military equipment may merit more expensive tags that can provide enhanced security.

Selective Blocking

This solution utilizes a special RFID tag known as a *blocker tag* to simulate the presence of a virtually infinite number of a subset of tags. This approach essentially blocks unauthorized readers from reading a subset of tags.

Selective blocking offers a versatile solution that minimizes some of the shortcomings of the previous techniques while avoiding the high cost associated with the more sophisticated solutions such as authentication and encryption. The combination of low cost and high security makes selective blocking an appropriate solution for implementing security in privacy sensitive consumer applications such as item-level tagging in retail stores[2]. In this case, consumers can use blocker tags to prevent all nearby readers from detecting and tracking tags attached to items *after* purchase. At home, the consumer may opt to destroy or disable the blocker tag so that other readers (for example, the refrigerator of the future we described earlier) can function properly.

Why is it easier to encrypt and secure wireless communication in cellular phone systems when compared to RFID systems?

There are two reasons for this:

1. **Cost:** In the case of cellular systems, the device generating data is a cellular phone. A cellular phone is a sophisticated device containing integrated circuits capable of performing encryption functions at a very low cost compared to the cost of the rest of the phone. In the case of RFID systems and the associated tags, the tags are essentially the computing devices that are attached to everyday items such as a box of cereal or a tube of toothpaste. The less expensive the item, the less sophisticated the circuitry in the tag must be to justify tagging that item. This, in turn, leads to very simple integrated circuits that cannot have the programmability feature to perform sophisticated encryption and authentication functions.

2. **Persistence:** Data exchange in a cellular phone communication happens in real-time. Data (voice) is generated, transmitted, and processed instantaneously and does not get stored or otherwise reused later. In this case, there is no need to safeguard against data being compromised at any time except during transmission. In the case of RFID systems, data is often persistent and is stored on a tag for interrogation and access. For maximum security protection and without compromising the utility of the RFID application, the tag and the reader must engage in an authentication protocol to ensure authorized access to the data on the tag. Again, this would require sophisticated circuitry on tags, which is not always affordable for low-cost objects being tagged.

---

[2] Blocker tags are not expected to be used widely until item-level tagging at the retail store level becomes prevalent. See Chapter 11, "Emerging Trends in RFID," for a discussion about item-level tagging.

Because the selective blocking technique requires writable tags, it cannot be successfully deployed in systems using read-only or chipless tags. The blocking technique can also be used maliciously by creating blocker tags that perform universal blocking or spoofing that can indiscriminately affect all readers within range and effectively mount a denial-of-service attack to disrupt the function of entire RFID systems. Although there are currently no commercially available solutions that can prevent or circumvent this problem, it is possible to build reader intelligence that detects spoofing problems and alerts an attendant.

Recommendations

No single security solution is suitable for every class of RFID application. In some cases, a combination approach may be necessary. For certain applications, security measures are specified by standards organizations such as ISO or EPCglobal, and are automatically available by compliant vendors. For example, ISO 15693—which applies to vicinity cards (smart identification cards)—specifies security measures related to tag data authentication, and is used for access control and contact-less payment applications.

Security, for RFID or otherwise, is a very complicated topic with challenging obstacles to overcome and complex solutions to implement. To deploy the most suitable scheme for securing RFID data in your application, we recommend that you do the following:

- Evaluate the unique advantages and disadvantages of all available solutions *in the context of your RFID project*.

- Consider the costs of implementing a particular security solution scheme.

- Weigh these costs against the risks and costs of vulnerability *in your RFID project*.

- Consult an RFID security expert or your trusted advisor vendor (discussed in Chapter 8, "Vendor Considerations and Landscape,") to help you with your decision.

Privacy Considerations

As we pointed out earlier, there are two basic ways that privacy can be compromized in the world. Thus far, our discussion has centered on the first—unauthorized third-party attacks and *breaches of security* that expose private and confidential data, thereby affecting businesses and/or individuals. Privacy may also be compromised through deliberate or accidental *misuse of data* by the very same entities—commercial or governmental—that collect and manage confidential data for legitimate reasons. This section discusses the latter situation, misuse of data, with particular emphasis on business-to-consumer relationships.

Although privacy concerns are not unique to RFID applications, specific features of RFID systems require businesses to be more aware of and sensitive to privacy issues. First, RFID is a relatively new technology that is frequently misunderstood by consumers. Second, RFID offers the potential to collect and track very significant amounts of data about consumers and their behavior, which can become a very powerful tool for abuse. Privacy concerns related to RFID revolve around questions of what is tracked, how it is tracked, and for what purposes it is tracked. We briefly outline the contours of these discussions while we try our best to avoid the fundamental and philosophical issues related to an individual's rights to privacy. We conclude this chapter with a discussion of how businesses can develop and implement RFID privacy best practices.

Consumer RFID Applications and Privacy

Consumer privacy groups worry about RFID primarily in relation to consumer applications (described earlier), contending that information collected could conceivably be used to track and trace people's actions and belongings in ways that could violate individual rights to privacy. These concerns are most frequently discussed by lawmakers and relayed by the press. The most Orwellian argument maintains that RFID technology itself invades privacy by creating an entirely new method of surveillance. Others argue that legislation should not focus on the technology, per se, but rather on the kinds of information governments and businesses are allowed to collect and what they are allowed to do with it.

Consumer Willingness to Disclose Personal Data

Although the discussions continue, consumers typically must first be willing to disclose personal or private data in order for a business to collect it. Most consumers are willing to do so, in varying degrees, in exchange for receiving certain benefits. Two general factors, purpose and trust, determine their willingness to do so.

Purpose

Consumers are generally willing to disclose personal data for receiving specific benefits. For example, many consumers are willing to provide details related to financial status and credit rating in order to qualify for a home loan. A study by Accenture[3], a large consulting firm, found that consumers trust their employers, banks, and health insurance providers with private data much more often than they do an online retailer or a supermarket. The same study found, however, that consumer concerns do not necessarily prevent sharing of personal information. Despite their stated concerns, 69% of the consumers surveyed said they are willing to exchange their personal data for cash, convenience, and bonus points.

Trust

Consumers usually disclose private data if they are relatively confident that the business *can* and *will* protect their data and use it only for a promised purpose. This element of trust facilitates the transfer of information and is bolstered by both the reputation of the business, legal mandates governing an enterprise's use of data, and a consumer's legal rights for the protection of such data.

The consumer that trusts the business with which she is working will likely have few privacy concerns. Interestingly, the aforementioned Accenture study found a wide gap between consumer perceptions and business perceptions of what factors engender and undermine trust. Whereas business respondents most frequently cited good customer service as the best way to engender trust, the majority of consumers cited company reputation or the length of their relationship with the business. In regard to factors undermining trust, 74% of business respondents cited online security fears, whereas 67% of consumers blamed aggressive marketing. More than half of those surveyed avoid dealing with companies whose privacy policies make them

---

[3] Accenture News Release, "Accenture Study Reveals Wide Chasm Exists Between U.S. Businesses and Consumers Regarding Privacy and Trust Related to Personal Data," Jan 2, 2004 at *http://www.accenture.com/xd/xd.asp?it=enweb&xd=_dyn%5Cdynamicpressrelease_691%.xml*.

uncomfortable. These findings underscore the importance for businesses to develop and adopt a framework for RFID privacy best practices.

RFID Privacy Best Practices

As previously noted, consumers do not share identical privacy protection preferences, and it is impossible to address all concerns of all consumers. The Internet provides a useful point of comparison as using it raises inherent privacy issues. Today, a number of consumers still refuse to conduct business over the Internet for fear of invasion of their privacy. Nonetheless, a critical mass of consumers who feel comfortable enough to conduct business over the Internet has emerged. As shown in Figure 10.2, retail e-commerce sales estimates in the United States show sales went from $7.4 billion in the third quarter of 2000 to $17.6 billion in the third quarter of 2004.

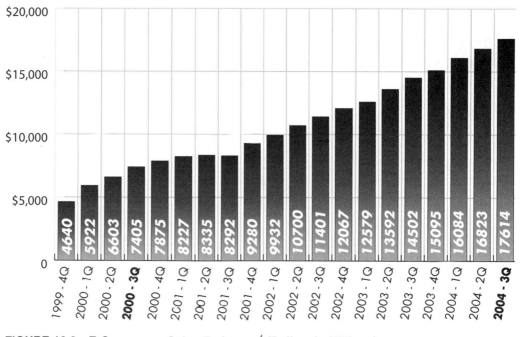

FIGURE 10.2   E-Commerce Sales Estimates[4] (Dollars in Millions)

[4] Source: The Census Bureau of the United States Department of Commerce (*http://www.census.gov/mrts/www/current.html*).

RFID technology advocates who share the goal of gaining consumer trust can assist expected growth and eventual ubiquity of RFID in the years to come. To this end, we describe a framework of RFID privacy best practices in the following sections.[5]

Education

Because RFID is a relatively new technology for most consumers, education programs about the technology, its uses, benefits, and limitations are important. For example, educating a consumer on the range limitations of RFID readers and the existence of transponder shields may reduce fears about Big Brother. At the same time, articulating specific benefits such as convenience, cost savings, and life-saving features of different RFID applications may give consumers the information required to make informed decisions that balance the benefits of an RFID application with its potential to violate privacy. For example, consider a scenario where a patient wearing an RFID bracelet in a hospital room is informed that the RFID bracelet can avoid life-threatening situations because it helps reduce the chance of medication error. This patient might then become less concerned about invasion of privacy associated with surveillance or access to her medical history.

Legislation

Legislation can play a big role in calming consumer fear of privacy rights violations. Knowing that the law limits the use of personal and private data is a powerful factor that can boost consumer confidence regarding protection of data. In the United States, several states (for example, California and Utah) have already introduced bills to address RFID privacy issues.

Disclosure

Disclosure is an important factor that creates a certain level of assurance for the consumer. A business using a consumer facing RFID system can provide such assurance to its customers by disclosing the following:

- Notification that the business is using RFID technology

- An explanation regarding the exact nature and details of why it is using RFID

---

[5] Because RFID shares many of the same privacy issues with the Internet, the best practices framework here reflects the spirit of more general privacy principles promoted by the European Union's Directive on Privacy and Electronic Communications, as well as the United States Department of Commerce Safe Harbor Framework.

- Statements about the specific personal data it does and does not collect

- Statements about how it will and will not use the data collected

- An explanation regarding how it protects data

- A statement about whether or not it will give this data to any other entity, and, if so, an explanation regarding the data use and protection policies of those entities

- References to any official, legal, or other types of privacy policies it follows

Consent

Simple disclosure of privacy practices and policies is generally not adequate. A trustworthy business should also seek the consumer's consent to collect and use her personal data. There are two types of consent: explicit and implicit. Explicit consent requires that the consumer explicitly agrees to having her personal data collected and used. Implicit consent essentially involves informing the consumer that by "using" the RFID system, she is giving consent to the collection/use of her personal data.

Seeking explicit consent can be difficult and/or impractical. For example, in a retail store where all items are tagged and consumer traffic is constant, it is impractical to seek consent on an ongoing basis or to remove RFID tags based on consumer consent. In such a case, entering a store may constitute a form of implicit consent, assuming the store has informed the consumer of this policy. However, there are further enhancements that can be made where explicit consent is not possible. The previously mentioned Mylar shielding bag that FasTrak supplies its users, allows drivers to place their tag inside the bag to avoid detection when they are not going through a toll plaza. In this scenario, removing the tag from the bag may be a form of implicit consent.

Summary

By addressing security vulnerabilities and implementing privacy protection practices, businesses can create mutually beneficial relationships with their partners, vendors, and customers while contributing to the eventual ubiquity of RFID.

RFID tags are tiny microchips that hold data. This data can directly or indirectly reveal confidential and private information about people or businesses that hold, handle, carry, or touch objects with RFID tags. Securing access to the data from unauthorized access and ensuring that the data is not used in a way that violates individuals' (or businesses') rights to privacy are critical. In this chapter, we focused on assessing security vulnerabilities of RFID systems, and we offered a set of solutions to help secure RFID data. The solutions we discussed vary in complexity and cost. Therefore, we recommended that such complexity and cost be weighed against the risks associated with security breaches.

When the ultimate ubiquity of RFID is realized, many items in the world will have an RFID tag on them whose data can be compromised. This poses a tremendous privacy risk—particularly, the risk of misuse by businesses or government agencies that have *authorized* access to the data. To address the issues associated with this risk, we offered a very specific set of privacy best practices that can help calm many of the concerns raised by consumers and privacy advocates.

The path ahead of RFID will include many discussions, debates, and subsequent solutions to address security and privacy issues associated with the proliferation of RFID. With this in mind, we move to the last chapter of the book, which discusses some of the more impact-full trends we expect to emerge from RFID technology and its applications.

11

EMERGING TRENDS
IN RFID

Five Questions This Chapter Will Answer

- What kind of advances in RFID tag design are expected?
- Are there any emerging computer hardware or software advancements that will help the deployment of RFID applications?
- Is item-level tagging a hype or a reality?
- What are the important catalysts for the widespread adoption of RFID?
- What does subcutaneous tagging have to do with RFID adoption in the enterprise?

The etymology of the word *trend* denotes both movement in a general direction as well as roundabout twists and turns. Early potters could not possibly have predicted the various turns the wheel would take during the 8,500 years after it was first invented. Similarly, it is unlikely that Michael Faraday could have imagined any of today's RFID applications when he discovered electromagnetic induction.

Technology trends, in particular, are not only shaped by technological invention and advancements but by economic, social, and political factors. These add a new dimension of complexity to predicting the ultimate disposition and acceptance of trends.

Keeping all these complexities in mind, we have identified the top emerging trends associated with RFID that are expected to drive its ubiquitous adoption. These trends fall into the following categories: Technological Advancements, Business Process Innovations, Evolving Standards and Legislation, and Consumer Application Innovations.

In this chapter, we use these categories as anchor to do the following:

- Take stock of where RFID technology stands today

- Discuss the recent innovations around RFID

- Examine key factors that will influence its evolution

Technological Advancements

Technological advancements are the high-octane fuel that powers the continued acceptance and growth of new technologies. These advancements can provide the following advantages:

- Make existing applications easier to use

- Offer more functionality

- Drive deployment costs down

Technological advancements open the door for new applications that were not imaginable or possible before. In the following section, we explore some of the more significant technological advancements that are under development today.

New and Improved Tags

Innovation around the design and manufacture of RFID tags is an ongoing process. Some of the most promising new designs are covered in the following sections.

Alternative Tag Designs

Many factors, including physical and environmental, affect the readable range and accuracy of tags. Some examples are detection near metal or liquid and extreme weather conditions such as low temperature or high humidity. Besides simply improving on existing technology to overcome these limitations, alternative physics are being employed that can sidestep or leapfrog these limitations.

The majority of the work in the alternative physics area includes developments around chipless tags, introduced in Chapter 3, "Components of RFID Systems." Chipless tags promise to improve upon the physical limitations of radio frequency detection while potentially offering reduced costs due to the absence of integrated circuitry. Chipless tags can be more easily applied near metal and liquid or embedded in items like paper, thereby offering greater flexibility and functionality with their use. One chipless tag technology showing promise in supply chain applications uses Surface Acoustic Wave (SAW) technology. SAW technology involves the propagation of radio frequency acoustic waves on the surface of polished crystals. Other promising chipless technologies that have the potential to revolutionize RFID applications use nanotechnology, genomics, or even chemistry to achieve chipless tagging and unique identification of objects such as paper currency and product labels. You can find vendors that develop and supply chipless tag technologies at this book's companion Web site, *www.rfidfieldguide.com*.

When it comes to major advancements in IC-based tag design, Smart Active Label (SAL) technology is gaining momentum in the market. SAL offers enhanced range and accuracy attributes while being less vulnerable to liquid or metal. A SAL tag is essentially a semi-active smart label with its power source in the form of a thin, flexible battery. Using SAL tags, tagging and detecting cans of soda and bottles containing liquid can become more practical and economical.

Tag Packaging

Tag packaging plays a significant role in the applicability and practicality of specific uses of RFID. Expect to see tag and antenna packaging designs that will continue to push the envelope of creativity and ingenuity, much as injectable and ingestible tags have done in the past. Chipless tags based on nanotechnology will certainly be at the forefront of such developments.

Another entirely different approach to tag packaging that is very promising is related to printed electronics. This involves the process of "printing" antennae, transistors, or even integrated circuits using conductive ink and standard printing processes. The potential to inexpensively print a tag onto a box or the packaging of an item unlocks a new set of possibilities for the widespread application of RFID in everyday items. Already, several companies (identified in the vendor guide at this book's companion Web site, *www.rfidfieldguide.com*) have designed smart label antennae that use conductive ink instead of copper.

Sensory Tags

Tags whose packaging integrates them with sensors can monitor, record, and even react to all sorts of environmental conditions. Known as sensory tags, these tag types promote an entirely new set of applications. The major advancements here will be around the coupling or combining of RFID tag technology with sensor technology in very small form factors. Smart Dust is one such combination that offers the functionality of tiny environmental sensors known as MicroElectroMechanical Sensors (MEMS) with active RFID tag-like capabilities. Each such device is expected to be one cubic millimeter in size. The potential applications of this technology span a wide area, from monitoring battlefield activities in a military operation to tracking the facial movements of the disabled to control their wheelchairs.

Architecture for the New Network

RFID systems generate mountains of new data that need to be synchronized, filtered, analyzed, managed, and acted upon, often in real-time or near real-time. Each tag is essentially a single computing device, albeit a very simple one, that acts as one node in a network of, eventually, billions or even trillions of such devices. This new network is dramatically different and in many ways more complex than even the Internet, the most complex network ever known. This fact is due primarily to the number of nodes that could exist in the expanded model of a worldwide RFID network, which will be several orders of magnitude larger than the number of nodes on the Internet. This simply means that traditional computing architectures and infrastructures will not be adequate to handle the dramatically higher data volumes expected in a network of RFID tags. Here, we discuss two different approaches under development that address the requirements of this new network from both hardware and software perspectives.

> ## Where will all this RFID data come from?
>
> Consider the scenario where a major retail chain will be tagging all its goods in all its stores, at the single item level. The number of tagged items in this scenario can easily reach 10 billion or more. This means that the data identifying the 10 billion items amounts to 120 gigabytes (10 billion × 12 bytes per tag). If these items were read once every 5 minutes somewhere in the supply chain, they would generate nearly 15 terabytes of tracking data every day (120 gigabytes × 12 times per hour × 10 hours per day). That's 15 terabytes of additional data generated by one retail chain every day. Using this formula, 10 major retailers tagging and tracking every item will generate 150 terabytes of data. This is bigger than the estimated 136 terabytes of data from 17 million books in the U.S. Library of Congress[1]. Obviously, a great majority of this RFID data is duplicate and will likely be discarded. However, all the data needs to be processed, examined, and acted upon, even if such action means simply ignoring much of it.
>
> We use item-level tagging (a more distant scenario) to demonstrate the eventual avalanche of RFID data. However, you can apply a similar formula to calculate the amount of data for a more immediate scenario: case- and pallet-level tagging. Although the volume of data in this case is an order of magnitude smaller, it still represents several orders of magnitude more data than a pre-RFID scenario.

Microprocessor Design

Several computer giants are revising their microprocessor development roadmaps in favor of a new microprocessor architecture called Chip Multi-Threading (CMT). One of the pioneers in this area is Sun Microsystems, which has already introduced the first design of this new architecture. This is just in time for the expected volume spike in RFID data as the U.S. Department of Defense (DoD) and major retailers around the world go into full deployment mode with their mandates. Simply put, CMT architecture bucks the trend of traditional microprocessor design and architecture that primarily seeks to perform single tasks faster and faster. Instead, CMT is an architecture that allows the efficient execution of many tasks simultaneously. This is *parallel computing* taken all the way to the core of the microprocessor.

---

[1] Source: University of California, Berkeley: How Much Information 2003? *http://www.sims. berkeley.edu/research/projects/how-much-info-2003/.*

Peer-to-Peer Computing

Although the data generated by RFID systems can easily reach trillions of bytes that need to be processed almost instantaneously, much of the data is disbursed across one or more enterprises, and often across the globe. This suggests that local processing of data, by RFID readers, before passing it along to a centralized computer can dramatically reduce the burden placed on centralized computing resources. This is an excellent scenario in which to apply Peer-to-Peer (P2P) programming techniques to perform RFID-related data processing locally. P2P technology is a type of distributed computing technique that decentralizes computing tasks across several less powerful cooperating computers (peers) within a network.

Expect RFID readers to become increasingly more "intelligent." Readers will perform many of the data processing, analysis, and management tasks within a local network of cooperating tags and readers. They will accomplish what today is mostly done by centralized computers.

Falling RFID Tag Price

With RFID technology, cost of components, especially cost of individual tags, will play a major role in determining its ultimate success and ubiquity. From an economic perspective, the cost of tags is expected to continue to drop as the volume production goes up to meet demand. However, both alternative chipless tag designs and advances in fabrication and manufacturing of integrated circuits (IC) are expected to drive the cost of tags dramatically lower. The *5 cents tag*, as it has been called, has been widely viewed as the inflection point where wide adoption of RFID will quickly occur. To be clear, the supply and demand equation alone is unlikely to drive the price of IC-based tags down to the 5 cents mark. Today, tag prices barely dip below 25 cents, even in high volumes. Therefore, alternative tag designs and more efficient tag manufacturing are likely to be important factors in driving the cost of tags down by another factor of five.

Business Process Innovations

As we've already discussed, for a technology to succeed and proliferate in today's world, it must be economically viable. In other words, it must enable businesses to meet one or more of their primary economic needs: reduce cost, increase revenue, and provide a competitive advantage. These objectives compel enterprises to innovate by examining existing business models and processes and reinventing or realigning them to fully take advantage of a new technology. The industry has just scratched the surface in business innovation that takes advantage of RFID technology.

Much of the impetus for future waves of innovation in RFID can be credited to the mandates set forth by major retailers around the world and the U.S. DoD. These mandates have created a ripple effect across the entire supply chain industry. Mandates have caused all supply chain partners including manufacturers, packagers, distributors, logistics and transportation agents, retailers, and wholesalers to examine ways in which they can improve the efficiency of their own supply chain systems.

RFID technology is already gaining good traction in certain areas of the supply chain such as warehouse management and inventory control. However, we are far from a fully integrated supply chain model. Although many technology and business leaders across supply chain enterprises agree that RFID offers tremendous promise, some argue that their short term return on investment (ROI) does not justify the initial cost of adoption—process re-engineering, re-tooling, and integration. Others are hesitant to make decisions without stronger standards, and most worry about privacy and related public relations issues. Despite these concerns, analysts have predicted tremendous growth for RFID in supply chain management during the next several years. For example, Venture Development Corporation expects the global shipments of RFID systems in manufacturing, logistics, and retail markets to reach $4 billion in 2007, up from $1.25 billion in 2004[2].

In the following sections, we examine the most critical business innovation trends in the supply chain. These will lead the way to RFID's ultimate deployment across the entire supply chain, starting with raw materials, all the way through to the checkout stand at your local retail store.

Item-Level Tagging

Item-level tagging is arguably the final frontier for RFID deployment. This concept permeates almost every type of supply chain application. However, from a practical standpoint, item-level tagging is fraught with challenges. On the consumer side, a number of security and privacy issues create concerns and will impact its pace of

---

[2] Source: Venture Development Corporation. Used by permission.

adoption. From the perspective of cost-effectiveness, the sub 5 cents tag will be key before the potential of item-level tagging can be realized. Although several pilots are under development already—for example, in large specialty retail and drug store outlets—expert and analyst opinion on the pace of adoption varies. Estimates of when item-level tagging at the retail store level becomes commonplace range between the years 2010 and 2020. Expect a slow but steady pace toward the item-level tagging of just about everything as the industry and consumers meet the challenges head on.

Third-Party Logistics Management

Retailers that are implementing RFID will have better and real-time visibility of the goods they carry in their stores. This, in turn, will help them become more efficient by enabling true real-time management of the links in the supply chain. Retailers may be able to eliminate their own distribution centers and receive goods directly from suppliers. Naturally, this will require suppliers to send goods more frequently, and in smaller quantities, directly to a larger number of retail stores, thereby shifting the equilibrium for handling and shipping costs. Expect third-party logistics (3PL) management services to include aggregation and distribution of RFID tagged goods. Major transportation and logistics companies such as UPS, as well as smaller specialized 3PL providers, will play a significant role in this area.

Real-Time Inventory Management

Inventory management happens at every level of the retail supply chain: at manufacture time, during transport, around distribution centers, and in warehouses, at both wholesale and retail levels. The recent mandates by major retailers will compel suppliers to continue to create new business models and applications that will not only help the retailers but the suppliers themselves, within their own four walls.

Expect a continuous stream of new applications in the inventory management area that offers new ways of making productive use of all the real-time RFID data. Applications already emerging—for example, from Checkpoint Systems, Inc.—include anything from real-time shipment processing and automated inventory updating at the distribution center to more effective merchandising and speedy point-of-sale operations at the retail store.

Business Intelligence

We've already seen how RFID enables access to lots of new data. The real value of this data is in leveraging it to make better business decisions. The capability to ask new questions or discover patterns in the data all provide more intelligence to a business, improve its decision-making capabilities, and help it become more competitive. Expect new data mining and analytics applications that help do that—by efficiently filtering and analyzing data that has never before been so readily available.

IT Outsourcing

Implementing RFID applications by definition means deploying expanded, or in many cases new, IT infrastructure. On the factory floor, in warehouses and distribution centers, in transportation vehicles, and in retail stores, new computers, applications, and RFID-specific components such as readers and antennae must be installed, integrated, and managed. The owners and operators of these facilities are not always ready and capable to handle this infrastructure by themselves. This creates many new IT outsourcing opportunities, particularly in the area of managed services. Expect an evolution of the already popular managed services model to include services that help manage RFID-related infrastructure and alleviate the need to duplicate new IT infrastructure where possible.

Real-Time Data Sharing for Total Supply Chain Integration

The highest level of efficiency in a supply chain occurs when information is shared in real-time between *all* the participants in the supply chain, not just between two immediate partners such as the supplier and the retailer. For example, consider a scenario where a retailer is running out of a particular type of sneakers. In a typical RFID application, the retailer would immediately detect this and order more sneakers from one of its suppliers. If the manufacturer of the sneaker also had access to this information, it could anticipate the demand and manufacture more of the same sneaker. Similarly, the supplier of the raw material would ensure availability of the appropriate material, and the shipping partner would have immediate visibility into when it would be expected to handle the transportation logistics. This might seem like a far-fetched example, and today it is. The problem to be solved here is not so much about RFID. It's more about the serialization, synchronization, and complex integration of data that needs to be shared among dozens of supply chain participants and partners. RFID has simply opened the door to facilitate this opportunity by making data more readily available and accessible. The recent RFID mandates in the retail industry and the EPCglobal standards for RFID in the supply chain are powerful catalysts that will continue to encourage enterprises to rethink their business models and deploy new processes and applications that extend the benefits of RFID to all their trading partners. Expect this scenario to develop gradually because the underlying economics are still evolving and improving, and the ultimate value proposition to businesses is often complex to articulate and implement.

Evolving Standards and Legislation

Standards and legislation will play a key role in shaping the future of RFID and its applications. In this section, we discuss the key trends related to them.

Industry Standards

As we discussed in Chapter 4, "Standards Related to RFID," EPCglobal established and supports the Electronic Product Code (EPC) Network as the worldwide RFID standard for immediate, automatic, and accurate identification of any item in a supply chain. Similarly, ISO has been developing RFID standards in several industries for two decades. Other local standards bodies and standardization initiatives are developing RFID-related standards in specific industries (for example, livestock), around certain technologies (for example, Smart Active Labels), and even relevant only to certain countries (for example, China). Although the move toward RFID standards definitely constitutes a trend, its evolution is far from complete. The process of developing standards is slow and includes review of opinions from industry participants. Vigorous and sometimes contentious debate and even opposing standards initiatives are often part of the process.

Government Regulations and Mandates

Government regulations regarding what items to monitor and report upon will serve as protections for entire industries or large populations. For example, tracking and reporting data about cattle might help to quickly isolate an outbreak of Mad Cow disease, potentially saving the livestock industry of an entire country. Similarly, tracking the pedigree of dangerous medication can prevent fraud and counterfeiting, potentially saving the lives of numerous patients. Because society as a whole is the beneficiary of these types of applications, expect government agencies to provide subsidies that will offset the costs incurred by individual businesses. Although individual businesses will indeed benefit from these applications, such benefits are often not always immediate enough to warrant voluntary investment by them.

Privacy Related Legislation

RFID's weakest link (from a supply chain perspective) exists between the retailer and the consumer. There are two reasons for this. First, a consumer does not necessarily have, or may not know of, a compelling reason to link one's identity or purchasing preferences and habits to the rest of the supply chain. Second, consumers may have compelling reasons not to share this information. There are a number of ways that enterprises can foster trust and ways that consumers can benefit from connecting to the supply chain, as discussed in Chapter 10, "Security and Privacy." We can expect continued discussion and debate around RFID privacy from consumer advocacy groups, vendors, and lobbyists. Governments will be pressed to impose new privacy legislation to calm consumer concerns. Their challenge will be to balance public and business interests.

Consumer Application Innovations

Consumer enthusiasm is a critical factor for the ultimate ubiquity of many technologies. The driving force behind creating such enthusiasm is application innovation that captures the consumer's interest and imagination.

In Chapter 1, "A Better Way of Doing Things," we described a number of RFID-enabled applications that directly benefit consumers. They include access control, people monitoring, electronic toll collection, payment and loyalty, patient care, sports timing, and many others. RFID and its applications are all around us, and innovations frequently occur. In April of 2004, VIP patrons of the Baja Beach Club in Barcelona, Spain, received syringe-injected RFID tag implants. This enabled them to pay for their drinks automatically, without reaching for their wallets—they also enjoyed free access to the VIP area and became permanently "cool."

Elsewhere, a company called RadarGolf has introduced tagged golf balls that can be easily located using a lightweight handheld RFID reader around the golf course.

Expect vendors to continue to capture our imagination and get us hooked on RFID by introducing interesting, creative, and original applications.

> ## Why subcutaneous tagging?
>
> Subcutaneous tagging, which involves injecting an RFID tag under the skin for identification and/or tracking purposes, is not a new concept. It has been used for identification of fish and domestic animals for more than a decade. However, innovative applications such as tagging club goers, and even tagging personnel to control access to sensitive offices or documents, leads to more consumer interest and enthusiasm, which in and itself will lead to a more receptive consumer psychology. You can only wonder how quickly subcutaneous tagging would take off if Britney Spears or Justin Timberlake decided to use it at their concerts as a means for purchasing memorabilia at a discount or for gaining backstage admission.

Summary

Thirty years ago, it was hard to imagine that anyone could do their Christmas shopping with a few clicks on a computer keyboard. Today, millions of people Christmas shop from the comfort of their personal computers at home. We now take for granted new conveniences of the Internet; using our computers to communicate with our peers half way across the globe or instantly selling shares of an underperforming stock we read about moments before. However, back in the 1960s and 1970s, computers were only used by corporate giants or governments to perform complex mathematical tasks. The concept of networks and the possibility of connecting computers together to help make everyday life more convenient was only a vision of a few elite computer scientists. They recognized the inevitable as a function of economic feasibility.

Now in a rapid growth phase, RFID technology holds similar promise and will become as ubiquitous in our everyday lives as the automobile or the wheels that move it. This will happen as RFID technology continues to provide an undeniable value proposition and helps reduce cost and increase revenues for businesses using the technology. Thus, the question of mass adoption of RFID becomes a matter of answering the following questions:

- Can RFID enable new profitable products and services?

- Can RFID help improve existing business functions and operations?

- Can RFID help increase competitive advantage?

- Can RFID provide more value-added services and products to the consumer?

The answer to all these questions is, of course, yes. Today, we are well underway toward the ubiquitous adoption of RFID technology. There are already hundreds of millions of tags used in our everyday life—from tags in our car keys to tags around our luggage handles. We use RFID technology when we enter our office buildings or when we pump gas. We use RFID in our hospitals and in marathon races. The next phase for RFID is adoption within the supply chain, the supply chain of anything that ends up in a retail store—bottles of cough syrup, boxes of cereal , children's toys, office equipment, furniture, and so on. The retail store is the last stop for true mass adoption of RFID technology. The journey there requires many steps and will take some time as the economics continue to become more favorable.

Ultimately, RFID will achieve its full potential, as have other great technologies. It will usher in a new economic, business, and consumer revolution much like the automobile did when in 1914, Henry Ford opened the world's first automobile assembly line and revolutionized the face of transportation as we knew it.

Appendix A

Case Study: Michigan Department of Agriculture

A Case Study on Tracking and Eliminating Tuberculosis (TB) from Animal Population with RFID Implementation

Courtesy: Michigan Department of Agriculture

The Client

The Animal Industry Division of the Michigan Department of Agriculture (MDA) is responsible for working with a statewide clientele of more than 15,000 beef and dairy producers (the producers) that raise approximately 1.1 million livestock animals. The livestock is worth close to $800 million.

The Challenge

Free movement and trade of healthy animals is the key to the profit and survival of the livestock business. If a cow cannot be traded in an auction market or sent to a slaughterhouse, the producer is unable to recoup the investment made in the material and infrastructure needed to raise and feed the cow. A widespread disease outbreak that kills the animals or requires the producer to depopulate his herd can have devastating consequences for an individual producer as well as other businesses that depend on healthy livestock industry for their income.

A few years back, the producers and the state of Michigan were looking at this stark scenario. After initial discovery of Tuberculosis (TB) in the tissue samples of a deer herd in Northern Michigan, the Michigan Department of Agriculture (MDA) found the disease present in beef herds in 13 northern counties of the lower peninsula of the state. This led to depopulation of several herds. The neighboring counties and states were also weary about the spread of the disease inside their borders over time. The disease spreads when a healthy animal comes in contact with the saliva or exhaled air of an infected animal—a situation common on farms as well as auction markets where animals share feed and drinking stations. In 2000, the United States Department of Agriculture (USDA), which was monitoring the situation and saw the growing spread of the disease, revoked Michigan's status as a TB-free state (for animals), triggering various restrictions on animal movements in and out of the Michigan counties. The restrictions included extra TB tests required for the animals, and added overhead per animal in terms of dollars and time spent compared to animals in TB-free states. Clearly, this was not conducive to business for the state's livestock industry.

To regain the TB-free status, the officials from MDA continued to test the livestock for TB in the affected counties, but they faced several issues. Because the number of animals testing positive was small compared to the number of total animals, it didn't make sense to depopulate them all or restrict movement of (ability to buy and sell animals) animals from all farms. To complicate matters, TB can remain dormant for a while before surfacing. An animal that tested healthy could, over time, develop TB. This meant uniquely identifying every animal and keeping a very accurate record of its movement. A typical bovine can change hands three times from birth to slaughterhouse. With the large number of animals involved, the paper-based tracking was turning out to be costly, time consuming, and prone to errors.

Faced with these challenges, the MDA looked at deployment of the National Farm Animal Identification Records (FAIR) program. RFID technology was seen as an enabler for this project.

Scope of the Project

The scope of the initial project, limited to the 13 affected counties, was to develop an Electronic Animal Identification (EID) system with the goal to identify all bovine (cattle) in the affected areas, and track and record their movement to eliminate infected animals. Successful completion of the project would restore Michigan's status as a TB-free state (for animals) over five years,[1] provided no more infected animals were found. Of the 15,000+ farms in the state, approximately 1,600 farms located in the affected 13 counties participated in the project. The farms contained approximately 70,000 animals. The project was implemented in four phases:

- *Phase 1*: Obtain and load animal farm location (premises) ID information into FAIR database.

- *Phase 2*: Develop an electronic data recording system, incorporating data from the old paper-based system.

---

[1] The TB-free status is not awarded right away because TB can remain dormant for a while. A 5-year period ensures that multiple generations of animals are tested and the ones with dormant TB are identified and eliminated.

- *Phase 3*: Record animal movement to and from markets and processing plants.

- *Phase 4*: Implement movement permit system to track animals as they moved from one place to another.

The USDA provided a grant for this project, which totaled $1.5 million over three years from 2001 to 2004. Most of this money was used to set up the requisite infrastructure for the project. Additionally, the MDA used its own people resources to test and record animals as well as manage the project.

Hardware and Software Products Used

- *National Farm Animal Identification Records (FAIR) program*: Holstein Association, a non-profit membership organization has tracked animal identification and pedigree information for decades and made it available to its members. It maintains a National FAIR program to enable animal identification and tracking. MDA partnered with National FAIR to use its model to develop the state's Electronic Animal Identification (EID) tracking system. This central database stores all the information about the animals, including their unique ID number, pedigree, TB test date, and test results.

- *Tags*: Close to 180,000 RFID tags made by Allflex were issued to producers at the cost of $400,000.

- *Handhelds, computers, and printers*: Fifty Psion handhelds were used as mobile readers at the cost of $120,000. Fifty computers were used at the cost of $50,000, and 30 printers were used at the cost of $9,000.

- *Stationary readers*: Readers and antennae made by Allflex were installed at various animal markets and slaughterhouses, averaging $10,000 per facility.

- *Movement Permit Application*: A Web-based application was developed, which, based on the animal ID number and certain qualifying questions, can check the FAIR database and, if appropriate, generate a movement permit for an animal that the producer can print on his computer. The permit is required at all animal markets and slaughterhouses in Michigan and surrounding areas.

The Solution: How It Works

The EID (Electronic Animal Identification) system consists of four components:

1. An RFID ear tag per animal, which sends the specific animal ID number to the reader.

2. *Readers*, which receive the signal from the tag and convert it into a unique number.

3. *Host computers*, which receive information from the reader and deliver to appropriate software program.

4. *Software*, which collects and analyzes the data.

For more information about how host computer and software interact, see Chapter 3, "Components of RFID Systems."

All animals are assigned a unique number using the American Identification Numbering (AIN) system. This number and the corresponding information about the animal are loaded in the FAIR database on an on-going basis. This data synchronization step is critical to the proper execution of the system. MDA officials armed with hand-held readers and computers ensure that the correct data is recorded. Farmers are also issued certain tags (with IDs) to be used on newborns. To date, approximately 180,000 RFID tags have been issued to animals on 1,600 farms in the affected counties.

To identify animals as they change hands, RFID readers are installed in 12 livestock auction markets in Michigan along with seven slaughter plants in Pennsylvania, Wisconsin, Illinois, and Michigan. The majority of Michigan's livestock passes through these facilities. As animals pass through the narrow animal alleys in these locations, the stationary readers mounted on the side read their IDs from the tags in their ears. These stationary readers can read tags up to 36" away (although the hand-held readers can read tags only 6" away). More than 33,000 animal identifications have been made at these facilities.

To further safeguard the system, the MDA requires movement permits for all animals, moving to any destinations. The system allows farmers to print the permits from their computers using a Web-based application. MDA can also fax a permit to a farmer who doesn't have access to the Internet. If an animal meets certain criteria, it is issued a movement permit. An animal without a permit is not allowed to be unloaded at the auction markets or slaughterhouses. After an animal is identified at these locations, the computers at these facilities update the animal's profile in the FAIR database with a new location. After an animal is slaughtered, the corresponding entry is removed from the database.

Results and Lessons Learned

- More than 33,000 animal identifications have been made since the start of the project. The accuracy of the handheld readers has been approximately 99% and tag retention has been over 96% (that is, the RFID tag stayed in the ear and was recovered at the market or slaughterhouses), higher than the retention rate for the typical metal tags. Approximately 1,600 farms in the affected counties (out of more than 15,000 farms in the state) have adopted RFID (a little over 10%). A total of 180,000 (estimated) tags have been issued so far.

- Twelve trace-backs have been achieved (that is, animals were traced back to their farm of origin). In May of 2003, an animal tested positive for TB outside of the affected counties. The entire history of the animal, including the farm of origin was traced within 15 minutes. In the past, such tracing would have been either impossible due to incomplete records or taken weeks to complete. The current process is fast enough to stop an infected animal from leaving the restricted area and pose a health hazard to other animals or humans.

- The computer and RFID-based process is more accurate, simpler to use, and easier to maintain than the paper-based system. As a result, 3.5 data entry positions have been saved. The current solution has also reduced the time it takes to retest a herd by 50%. It prevents wrong animals from being tested and possibly killed.

- The resulting superior tracking and elimination of infected animals has enabled Michigan to make progress towards regaining its TB-free status. The progress has ensured continued access to markets for Michigan producers. Over time, such traceable meat can even be marketed at a premium, increasing profits for the producers.

- Successful execution of this project has enabled MDA to lay the groundwork for deploying EID in the rest of the state. The blueprints of this project can also help other states replicate Michigan's success. A cooperative effort is already underway between the government and the industry in the form of The U.S. Animal Identification Plan (USAIP). It is chartered to define the standards and framework for implementing and maintaining a national animal identification system for the U.S. As part of the project, USDA has established a National Animal Identification Development Team with participation from more than 70 animal associations, organizations, and government agencies. A fully implemented plan could identify all premises that had contact with a foreign animal disease within 48 hours after discovery.

Case Study: Sun Microsystems

A Case Study on RFID Usage in an Inventory Tracking Pilot

Courtesy: Sun Microsystems

The Client

With more than $11 billion in annual revenue, Sun Microsystems is a leading provider of industrial strength computing systems consisting of server, software, storage, and services. The company prides itself on providing innovative solutions to its customers that reduce computing complexity and lower the overall cost of ownership of computing infrastructure for its customers.

The Challenge

Because Sun designs and builds the majority of its servers, efficient supply chain and manufacturing systems are critical in keeping its operational costs down. Higher operational costs can either make the product less competitive or hurt margins. The company has maintained an on-going focus on streamlining its operations and pursued an aggressive program for process improvement, modeled after the Six Sigma methodology.

Some time back, Sun's manufacturing plant in California was looking at various ways to further streamline its operations. This plant was responsible for making some of Sun's mid-range servers and storage systems. Although the manufacturing and sourcing were highly streamlined, it seemed to the plant supervisors that the processes for overall inventory tracking could be improved. RFID technology seemed to be an enabler for this. At the same time, Sun was quite deeply involved in the emerging area of RFID technology through its leadership role in developing standards, as well as middleware software, for RFID. It seemed that a hands-on RFID project to improve internal operations would help Sun stress test the newer versions of its software and create an internal competency of RFID solution architecture and deployment. With these benefits in mind, the company decided to deploy an RFID pilot in its manufacturing operations.

Sun faced several challenges in the selection and design of the RFID pilot. Manufacturing of a mid-range server, the type being manufactured at this plant, requires many distinct steps such as component assembly, testing of sub-assemblies, software installation and customization, and testing of the final product. A pilot that puts RFID tags on every sub-assembly of a machine would require major changes to the manufacturing process and as a result, was considered out of scope. There was another issue as well. Because the pilot would have a fixed start and stop date, followed by a review and possible process improvement phases, if Sun started tagging its production machines during the pilot phase, some customers would have machines with RFID tags and others would not (after the pilot ended). Sun needed to find a pilot in which the tagged objects would remain inside its factories (also known as a closed loop process) and still provide meaningful enough results to make extrapolations about operational savings of a fully deployed RFID system. It found the perfect pilot in its Rotational Capital Process.

What Is Rotational Capital Process?

Testing a mid-range server (multiprocessor) requires a variety of test components and equipment, including other servers, server chassis, and various I/O cards. The testing could occur at multiple stations during the assembly, and may require more equipment than typically available in the test harnesses at that station. For example, to test a CPU board for a multiprocessor server, a server chassis with a certain configuration of disk drives, memory, power supplies, and CPU boards may be needed. If the right configuration were not available, an operator would borrow the missing items from a pool of capital equipment (known as rotational capital). When the testing was completed, the borrowed capital equipment would be returned to its original location. In this manner, the capital equipment can rotate in and out of the pool.

Though an ERP system-based tracking process was in place for the rotational capital, it was not working well. Sometimes, the operators forgot to return the equipment or made a mistake in entering the data into the ERP system. As a result, data synchronization–reconciliation of data between what was physically available and what was in the ERP system–was an on-going challenge. Several people were working full-time to resolve the arising discrepancies by going around the plant looking for missing equipment and bringing them back to their proper location. Because these were high-value items, the labor cost was justified in terms of not having to keep excessive test inventory.

Scope of the Project

The scope of the project was limited to showing the viability of using RFID technology in an environment with high metal content, and gaining positive ROI (return on investment). It was broken into several steps:

1. Define use cases based on existing process discovery

2. Define the architecture and source components

3. Build the pilot, including any custom software and physical setup

4. Deploy the pilot for three months

5. Evaluate the results

A virtual team, consisting of members from the manufacturing operations, Sun Professional Service architects, and engineers from the RFID software team was put together to drive the project. Appropriate management approvals were obtained and budget was secured to conduct the pilot. Because the goal was to create a system that can be rolled out across Sun's supply chain, a standards-based deployment was required. The team decided to use EPCglobal's UHF specifications to ensure such compliance. The software components were already compliant with Java and Jini standards.

Hardware and Software Products Used

- *Tags*. UHF tags made by Alien Technology (I-tag).

- *Readers*. Stationary readers and linear antenna from Alien Technology.

- *RFID Middleware*. Sun EPC Event Manager.

- *EPC Information Server*. Sun EPC Information Server.

- *Tracking Application*. A custom built tracking application was used to keep a record of location histories of each item and a log of all transactions.

- *Reporting*. Brio reporting tool.

- *Database*. Oracle.

- *Application Server*. Sun JES Application Server.

The Solution: How it Works

The pilot system consists of four components:

1. *An RFID tag* per unit of test equipment, containing its EPC, which uniquely identifies it.

2. *Readers and antennae*, which receive signals from the tags and map them to specific entries in the equipment database.

3. *RFID middleware*, which receives information from the reader, filters it, and delivers to the appropriate software program.

4. *Business processing software*, which collects and analyzes the data.

For more information about how these different components interact, see Chapter 3, "Components of RFID Systems."

First, all the test equipment was tagged with Alien Technology's UHF I-tags. Because quite a few items had heavy metal content, the tags were affixed on top of a plastic, which was attached to the metal. Linear antennae were chosen due to their enhanced read performance, requiring that tags be vertically aligned to the antennae. The tags were carefully placed to ensure this orientation. Each tagged object was associated with an EPC and entered into the corresponding Oracle database repository.

The pilot layout was created such that the operators taking equipment from the central location to their station or vice-versa passed through a reader gate. The tagged object(s) were identified at this location. The operators were trained to verify the data read by the reader, manually override any inaccuracies, if needed, and complete the transaction. The transaction triggered several events. For example, the location of this object would change in the central repository and the transaction logs would be updated. When the testing was done, the whole process occurred in reverse, whereby the material going through the reader gate was now added to the inventory.

Due to the scope, budget, and duration of the project, the list of tagged equipment in the database was not synchronized with the master list of equipment in the database. It should be noted that such integration would surely be covered in the full deployment.

Results and Lessons Learned

The pilot showed that it was possible to track and trace items with heavy metal content using standardized tags and RFID middleware. Here are some of the findings:

- The accuracy of the system was quite high, approximately 99.5%.

- Operator training turned out to be an issue. The tags were read properly as long as the operators walked through the RFID gate, which did not always happen.

- Linear antennae provided much better response than circular antennae. Tag orientation vis-à-vis the reader was proved critical in such situations.

- Although the pilot project touched upon a very small part of the overall supply chain and manufacturing processes, the ROI analysis showed that if fully implemented, the project would have a positive ROI over a three-year horizon, with break-even point in approximately 2 years.

- Handheld readers were desirable as they could help track inventory in situations where operators took the test components without passing them through a stationary RFID gate.

Case Study: Operation Enduring Freedom / Operation Iraqi Freedom (OEF/OIF)

A Case Study on Support of U.S. Military Operations in Afghanistan & Iraq

Courtesy: Savi Technology

Savi's Client

U.S. Department of Defense (DoD), U.S. Central Command, and the U.S. Army Program Manager—Automatic Identification Technology (PM-AIT).

Client's Investment

Since 1994, the DoD, through PM AIT, continues to award multi-year procurement contracts to Savi Technology to provide Radio Frequency Identification (RFID) transponder tags; fixed, portable and handheld readers; and associated hardware, software and professional support. These near real-time solutions enable Total Asset Visibility (TAV) for the DoD. In addition to its own products, Savi provides all forms of RFID products and solutions through a full spectrum of RFID partners. The value of the three IDIQ contracts exceeds $250 million.

Client's Top Requirement: Total Asset Visibility (TAV)

The genesis of using RFID to obtain TAV came from the inability during Desert Shield and Desert Storm to know the contents of containers and track and locate supplies in the DoD supply chain. Over 40,000 containers were shipped to the Gulf, with redundant materiel and supplies resulting in enormous "iron mountains" of containers staged in ports and holding yards. At least two-thirds of these containers had to be opened to see what was inside.

> **"During the Gulf War, we simply did not have good information on anything. We did not have good tracking; we had no real asset visibility. Materiel would enter the logistics pipeline based on murky requirements, and then it could not really be tracked in the system.... We lacked the necessary priority flows to understand where and when things were moving. It was all done on the fly, on a daily basis... It truly was brute force.**

Generally speaking, if front-line commanders weren't sure of what they had or when it would get there, they ordered more... The result was the oft-referenced "iron mountains" of shipping containers. We had too much, and, worse yet, we did not know what was where."

—USAF Gen (ret.) Walter Kross Director of Ops & Logistics of the U.S. Transportation Command during the "first" Gulf War

To prevent a recurrence of these inefficiencies and lack of visibility, the U.S. Army, through its Logistics Transformation Agency (LTA) and PM AIT worked diligently to install a worldwide RFID infrastructure, called the DoD In-transit Visibility (ITV) Network.

The DoD ITV Network is comprised of more than 800 locations with over 1,300 read and write stations to track and locate the flow of military supplies and equipment ranging from boots and food to bullets and missiles through the supply chain—both in times of peace and conflict. The DoD ITV network is the world's largest active RFID system that tracks and locates over 300,000 shipments per year in near real-time throughout the global DoD supply chain. In January 2003, the United Kingdom (UK) Ministry of Defence (MOD) elected to extend a like capability throughout the UK MOD supply chain. In November 2003, the DoD Joint Chief of Staffs J4 offered to extend the use of the DoD ITV network to all Coalition Allies.

RFID Comes of Age and Proliferates

As the DoD and Army's operational tempo (OPTEMPO) increased in recent years, so too did the use of RFID tagging of containers and Air Lines of Communication (ALOC) pallets. In March 2001, the DoD ITV system recorded 3,148 tag reads by interrogators. In March 2002 more than 28,000 tag reads occurred; however, this massive growth only served as a sentinel of much greater volumes to come. With the deployments and operations in support of Operation Enduring Freedom (OEF) and Operation Iraqi Freedom (OIF) in 2002 and 2003, the tag reports exploded to more than two million tag reports in March 2003. The DoD's explosive growth in the use of Savi's RFID tags, interrogators, other products and services was fueled by the U.S. Central Command's demand for visibility of all materiel and supplies being shipped to support OEF and OIF. As a result of this demand, the use of the ITV network came of age as a standard for end-to-end supply chain visibility. The benefits from the use of

Savi's technology are well documented; however, the OEF and OIF "lessons learned" show that many more returns are yet to be realized from total integration and institutionalization of the near real time event data into the DoD's logistics systems.

How It Works

Through the use of Savi's technology, along with other technology providers, the DoD installed a worldwide RFID infrastructure and network to track and locate materiel and supplies moving through the vast, complex, and multi-national end to end supply chain. The DoD TAV network uses linear and two-dimensional barcodes, optical memory cards, active RFID tags, and GPS systems to track tri-walled shipments, commercial and ALOC pallets, and ISO containers through over 800 checkpoints in more than 45 countries.

Asset tracking begins with the aggregation of item data to case contents, to pallet configuration to visibility inside the shipping container to shipment units in a truck, plane or ship. The DoD uses Savi's active, data-rich battery-powered tag to provide "in the box," nodal, "on demand" and "between node" visibility. The "between node" occurs when Savi's RFID tags are coupled with satellite and GPS technology. The Savi RFID tags can store up 128KB of data (80 pages of text).

The DoD created its own format for the Savi tag. The TAV format provides license plate data, detailed commodity information, and specific transportation transactions. The DoD shipper uses their existing logistics systems coupled with Savi's TAV Tools and Unisys' Transportation ITV Processing (TIPS) software and Savi's Tag Docking Stations (TDS) to write the TAV data to the RFID tag. The write record is automatically sent from the TDS to the DoD TAV servers in the U.S., Europe, Korea, and Southwest Asia. As the RFID tagged shipments travel through the DoD supply chain, the RFID tag identification (ID) number is automatically collected by Savi's RFID interrogators. The RFID tag IDs are automatically associated with the interrogator's ID and location and all three data elements are automatically routed to the appropriate DoD TAV server. In addition, at some sites and for some DoD systems, tag data is extracted and automatically populated to existing DoD logistics systems. Through this automatic and near real time data collection, the DoD logistics operators can see the arrival and departure of shipments at any of the over 800 locations. In addition, if there is a crucial requirement to locate a specific item at any of the nodes, the logistics operator can query the TAV system to find all the locations where the item is located.

Finally, and probably most importantly, logistic operators can use Savi's handheld interrogators to send a query to a RFID tag on a shipment to gain "in the box" visibility without opening the container. Lastly, when required by operational necessity, the RFID tags when coupled with satellite and GPS, can provide "between node" visibility. Deployed units in OEF, OIF, and other locations use Savi's Mobile RFID Flyaway Kits, also called Early Entry Deployment Support Kits (EEDSK), to provide RFID infrastructure in contingency operational areas. The EEDSK contains handheld interrogators to read RFID tags, satellite phones for network connections, and solar panels to generate power to allow connection to the DoD TAV servers.

"Precision-Guided Logistics" in OEF/OIF a Quantum Leap in Efficiency

The application of RFID tracking technology in OEF and OIF benefited war fighters by allowing them to have unprecedented real-time visibility and dynamic routing and management of supplies—a quantum leap over a decade prior.

Numerous accolades came from OEF and OIF logisticians and combatants for the "in the box," "on demand," and "nodal" visibility for materiel and supplies. By using handheld interrogators, users could instantly locate needed supplies such as milk or water or avoid opening unmarked containers holding hazardous materials.

Perhaps the bottom line on the cost savings attributable to ITV and RFID-enabled achievements lies in the fact that during OIF 30 percent fewer troops were deployed than in Desert Storm; however, the Army used 90% fewer shipping containers. The use of the RFID tags and the DoD TAV network significantly contributed to the reduced container usages as well as facilitated port clearance and rapid processing of materiel and supplies through theater distribution centers to ultimate consignees. During OIF, USAF GEN John Handy, U.S. TRANSCOM Commander remarked: "In Desert Storm, we had mountains of containers that never even got opened the whole time we were there. That's not happening this time, and that kind execution of our business will be a significant part of the success of the mission." The significance of TAV to mission success was pointed out by John Osterholz, Director of Architecture and Interoperability in DOD's Chief Information Officer's office. Mr. Osterholz noted that the use of RFID enabled the United States to be fully prepared for war in half the time it took to gear up for Desert Storm, and allowed users to "dive deep" into the information flow and quickly get items to the units that needed them.

"Whereas during the first Gulf War when we did most of our logistics tracking on paper. This time, with improvements in the tags, readers as the lynchpin of whole information, and software systems to create holistic solutions at the strategic and tactical levels simultaneously, there was in-transit visibility of things that were moving available to certified users—right on the Web.

DoD now has clear knowledge of when things are actually going—the planes, the ships, what's going to be on them, what needs to be moved. TRANSCOM has gone digital and this represents a quantum leap in capability and efficiency from the first desert War. Our operators now get ground truth at ground zero—and everywhere else. And we now have the technology to absorb and to manage and precisely guide materiel."

—USAF Gen (ret.) Walter Kross Director of Ops & Logistics of U.S. Transportation Command during the "first" Gulf War

A true boots-on-the-ground perspective on the dramatic efficiency gains associated with the advent of "precision-guided logistics" was provided by U.S. Army Major Forrest Burke, Chief of Logistics Information Management, Coalition Forces Land Component Command (CFLCC). Said Major Burke: "What would have taken several days to locate in the first Gulf war, we can now find in 20 minutes. Back in 1991, I had a clipboard and carbon paper." According to the National Defense Transportation Association, which honored Savi with its 2003 National Transportation Award in September, "Savi Technology has demonstrably advanced the art and science of defense transportation by providing the DoD the technology to move away from brute force logistics (large stockpiles of materiel) in the operational theater and toward the precise delivery of materiel to the required location at the right time."

U.S. Forces... and Beyond

As mentioned earlier, in addition to the deployment of its RFID solutions within the U.S. Department of Defense, OIF also saw Savi Technology's hardware and software successfully leveraged in support of British forces within the Coalition. The U.K.

MOD noted that it recouped its multi-million dollar investment in the technology within two weeks of implementation just prior to OIF. Tracks for tanks were urgently needed in the theater, and the UK MOD was about to lease the costly *Antonov*—the world's largest air cargo plane—to transport the equipment from the UK to the Middle East. However, after querying the TAV network, British forces found tank tracks with affixed RFID tags already in theater, thus saving the substantial cost of leasing the aircraft for an expedited shipment.

Building on Success: the DoD RFID Mandate

Based on the logistics tagging and tracking successes of OEF/OIF, on October 2, 2003, the U.S. Department of Defense (DoD) announced a policy to institutionalize and extend the use of Savi's data-rich active RFID products across the Department to include shipments from DoD vendors. This innovative and overarching RFID policy includes the mandated use in early 2005 of the new Electronic Product Code (EPC) passive RFID tags for product, case lot, and pallet identification and location. During 2004, the DoD will conduct several prototypes to demonstrate the how the EPC can be used to add additional asset visibility for DoD's supply chain. The EPC when coupled with Savi's active RFID tags will allow the DoD to gain the much sought after automatic nested visibility to alleviate many of the issues identified as part of the "last ugly mile." Fulfilling the "nested visibility" mandate, according to DoD, is "critical" to logistics transformation and will help to "improve business functions and facilitate all aspects of the DOD supply chain." The new RFID policy and the corresponding RFID tagging/labeling of DoD materiel are applicable to all items except bulk commodities such as sand, gravel or liquids. The policy will require suppliers to put passive RFID tags on the lowest possible piece part/case/pallet packaging by January 2005, and immediately affix active, data-rich RFID tags to higher-level assets such as air pallets, containers, equipment and transport modes. DoD has been the primary catalyst for development of state-of-the-art RFID and with this mandate will stimulate even further advancements both throughout the armed forces and the commercial supply chain. In promulgating the policy, the DoD continues to demonstrate its global leadership and foresight in accelerating wider adoption of RFID technologies for supply chain applications. Savi Technology is proud and privileged to have worked closely with the DoD for nearly a decade in designing, developing and providing data-rich active RFID tags, readers and support software. Savi is fully committed to taking lessons learned from OIF to develop the next generation of RFID-enabled solutions that extend the breadth and depth of real-time, total asset visibility of military supplies in times of peace and conflict. By continuing to work with partner solutions, Savi is committed to being the "on ramp" to the TAV system by "nesting" its solutions with EPC-compliant tags and other technologies for both end-to-end and top-to-bottom visibility.

About Savi

Savi is the proven leader in global supply chain security and real-time asset management with over 14 years of logistics infrastructure experience. Founded in 1989, Savi Technology is headquartered in Sunnyvale, California, with offices in Hong Kong, Johannesburg, London, Brussels, Singapore, Taipei, and Washington D.C.

Case Study: Woolworths, Plc.

A Case Study on Reducing Shrinkage and Theft in the Supply Chain with Savi's Asset Management System and RFID Implementation

Courtesy: Savi Technology

Special Note:

In 2003, Woolworths won a prestigious European Retail Solutions Award in the category of *Supply Chain Solution of the Year*. Judged by a panel of European retailers, this award recognizes those outstanding retailers who have successfully implemented new information technology (IT) to drive their business forward both economically and operationally. This case study discusses their new award-winning implementation.

Challenges Facing Woolworths Leads to "The Chipping of Goods Initiative"

Woolworths' success depends on its ability to respond to increasing consumer demands. But like most global retailers, Woolworths experiences problems with product "shrinkage" due to lack of asset visibility in the supply chain. Shrinkage problems are due to: incorrect shipment deliveries, stock losses in the distribution center and theft of goods in transit and from the stores themselves. These problems resulting from lack of asset visibility within the supply chain cause many large High Street retailers to lose tens of millions of pounds per year.

Based on these challenges, Woolworths has looked into various measures to resolve their supply chain visibility issues. One such measure is a project based on the introduction of real-time tracking and tracing of goods using radio frequency identification tags.

The project is part of the Chipping of Goods initiative, sponsored by The Home Office to demonstrate how RFID can reduce shrinkage and theft. The Chipping of Goods Initiative is a program that supports innovative demo projects to reduce theft and loss in the supply chain.

Key Technologies for Woolworths' Asset Visibility

Two key technologies were selected to address the problems Woolworths faced: RFID technology and asset management software provided by Savi Technology.

Savi Technology is the proven leader in providing of supply chain asset management, security and collaboration software that is uniquely integrated with automatic data collection and identification systems to provide real-time logistics solutions.

Scope of Initial Project

The initial project was installed at the Primary Woolworths Distribution Center in Swindon, Wiltshire, England. Various other Woolworths retail outlets that are serviced by the Swindon Distribution Center are also set-up with the RFID technology. A total of 900 retails sites across the United Kingdom have been defined for implementation and so far 90 sites have been enabled for the demo project.

The key goal of the project was the integration of Bar Codes, Active RFID and GPS systems into a single supply chain visibility solution.

The implementation from May 2002 to February 2003 included the following Savi products:

Savi Software Products

- *Savi Asset Management System*—A full-featured, Web-based software application for managing the complete life-cycle of critical supply chain assets such as dollies, totes, trailers, intermediate bulk containers, pallets and other types of high value mobile assets.

- *Savi SmartChain Platform*—SmartChain is a distributed logistics platform that collects, aggregates and processes data in real-time.

- *Savi Site Manager*—The data is sent to SmartChain from the Savi Readers via the Savi Site Manager. Site Manager provides a local point of presence for data collection.

Savi Hardware Products

- *Savi SR-600 Readers*—Savi's fixed Readers have been placed at Woolworths stores to monitor tag activity and communicate tag location and data to the Savi SmartChain platform.

- *Savi SP-600 Signposts*—A total of thirty Savi Signposts have been placed at various distribution centers. Signposts activate tags within their vicinity for enabling precise identification of tagged items at specific locations.

- *Savi ST-602 Tags*—A total of 15,200 Savi Tags have been placed on Woolworths, Plc. containers. The ST-602 tags are small (6.2 cm x 4.3 cm x 1.2 cm), and mountable with dual short range and long range frequency transmission.

- *Savi SMR-640P Mobile Readers*—A total of fifteen Savi Mobile Readers— mobile, lightweight, battery operated reader modules used with an off-the-shelf Personal Digital Assistant (PDA) to commission, identify and configure the Savi Tags—are being used by Woolworths personnel.

The Savi Series 600 components (Readers, Tags, and Signposts) are built on Savi's innovative EchoPoint technology. Savi's EchoPoint technology is a new, innovative technology that uses two operating frequencies. EchoPoint combines long-range communication (at 433.92 MHz) with precise spot-level locating (at 123 kHz and 132 kHz).

The Solution: How It Works

The RFID supply chain solution developed for Woolworths integrates a comprehensive set of technologies, and provides visibility of conveyances and items throughout the warehouse and retail delivery system. This begins with Savi's Series 600 RFID hardware -Tags, Signposts, and Readers, which communicate through Savi's Site Manager to the Savi SmartChain platform and Savi Asset Management System.

It starts with Savi RFID tags on each dolly, and a real-time integration with Woolworths order picking and packaging systems. With the RFID tag identification, Woolworths can identify the location of goods ordered by a store within the distribution center, and track the deliveries, from the picking area, to the marshalling area, Goods-Out bay, Trailer, and to the actual store—complete with a Proof-of-Delivery (POD) delivered wirelessly from the remote store at the time of the delivery.

Within the warehouse distribution center, goods are picked to order and collected in a number of totes. The totes are loaded onto tagged dollies. A real-time interface matches the tote barcode and dolly RFID signals. Later the assembled dolly is moved to a marshalling area where it waits to be aggregated on a trailer route. Route plans sent to the customized Savi system allow the system to determine whether dollies are being loaded onto the correct trailer, and if not, an audible and visual LED messaging system indicates the errant dolly immediately. When the trailer is ready to depart, the system downloads the trailer manifest to a new handheld terminal for drivers, which is fitted with the Savi SMR-640 Mobile Reader module.

As the truck with trailer travels along its route, its position can be dynamically displayed on the Transport Management Centre (TMC) system from Microlise. When the driver has completed the delivery, the POD data, along with GPS, and seal status information, is transported from the remote trailer over a wireless wide area network back to the primary distribution center through the TMC.

At the distribution center, the TMC uploads the information to the Savi Site Manager, which then passes the data along to the Savi SmartChain Platform where it is aggregated and processed. At any time during this process, personnel may view the asset, order, or trailer seal status, and asset location, through their Web browser with the Savi Asset Management System.

Unlike bar codes, RFID tags do not require line of site, and the data stored on them can be updated at various points throughout the supply chain. By associating the orders packed within each tote bin to the RFID tag on the dolly on which they are stacked, Woolworths gains complete visibility of stock movement.

From the mobile terminal POD information, or from fixed RFID readers installed at high volume stores, the system is able to determine if the dollies and associated items in totes have been delivered to the correct store. In the case of stores using fixed technology, this is done instantaneously as the goods are delivered. If the dolly is mis-delivered, a real-time alert is sounded. To complete the cycle, Savi's fixed signposts and readers are installed at Woolworths Goods-In and Tipping bays to detect the return of empty dollies.

In larger stores, Savi Series 600 equipment has been installed in the goods inwards loading bays. With this system, no user intervention is necessary. Savi 600 Hardware reads the RFID tags as the dollies are unloaded from the vehicle and checks these dollies off against the expected manifest of goods. The data is transmitted back to the Swindon Distribution Centre in real-time using SmartChain and Savi Asset Management System software on a local computer. Again, if dollies are incorrectly unloaded, the driver is informed by flashing lights and a warning siren.

The implementation described here is the first system of its type anywhere in the world combining Bar Codes, Active RFID and GPS in a single supply chain visibility solution. The combination of these technologies was considered by the judges of the European Retail Solutions Awards to be a key factor in selecting Woolworths' implementation as Supply Chain Solution of the year. Woolworths Plc. was commended for the broad scope of integrating these technologies across the supply chain.

Return on Investment (ROI)

The Chipping of Goods Initiative covers only a small proportion of the goods delivered from the Woolworth's Swindon distribution center to the stores. Even though this is a limited trial, it is envisaged that if the same technology were to be rolled out over the full distribution infrastructure a reduction in the order of 10% would see the system pay for itself in the first year.

The Key Benefits: Complete Supply Chain Visibility & Increased Revenue

Woolworths has benefited on many levels through the Chipping of Goods Initiative and RFID implementation. With the new RFID Supply Chain solution and Savi Asset Management System, Woolworths can now track conveyances and goods throughout the retail distribution system. This will help reduce shrinkage through increased visibility and audit trails. Reduced shrinkage and theft means increased profit margins.

Previously, without accurate knowledge of mis-delivered goods, out-of-stock situations could result in lost sales. Now the increased visibility will help prevent mis-routing and mis-deliveries, and will allow store inventory balances to be better managed.

Other benefits to Woolworths include:

- Improved goods distribution will minimize costs and increase top line revenue
- Increased profit margins means increased shareholder value—stock prices will go up
- Elimination of incorrect deliveries of dollies to the stores involved
- Successfully tracking goods between warehousing and in-store

- Control over the storage and transportation of their goods

- Assurance of a reliable and secure transport system for every shipment—every time

In the future, Woolworths expects that RFID systems will play a significant role in the control and tracking of their goods—nationwide.

About Savi

Savi is the proven leader in global supply chain security and real-time asset management with over 14 years of logistics infrastructure experience. The company's broad customer base includes the U.S. Department of Defense as well as numerous international ports, terminal operators, carriers, asset owners and third-party logistics providers. Founded in 1989, Savi Technology is privately held, with headquarters in Sunnyvale, California and offices in Hong Kong, Johannesburg, London, Singapore, Taipei, and Washington D.C.

Case Study: Smart & Secure Tradelanes—Phase One Review

A Case Study on Leveraging Security and Efficiency in Today's Global Supply Chains via Network Visibility

Courtesy: Savi Technoloy (Based on "Network Visibility: Leveraging Security and Efficiency in Today's Global Supply Chains" whitepaper)

> *"The U.S. government needs to focus not merely on security, but all the other economic benefits and efficiency gains enabled by implementing systems like SST—which can dramatically decrease costs in the global supply chain."*
>
> *—SST Phase One logistics service provider*

Introduction

Smart and Secure Tradelanes (SST) is an industry-funded supply chain security and efficiency initiative. It was founded on the premise that the considerable gaps in global supply chain security put prosperity, free trade, and economic development at risk. These gaps pose the real risk that a terrorist event could lead to a shutdown of ocean ports and a strangling of trade. While industry has become acutely aware of the threat posed by the potential use of a weapon of mass destruction, any source of mass disruption poses an equally grave threat to efficient trade.

SST is a unique and ambitious initiative. Among its distinctions are that it is:

1. *Industry-directed and funded,* which demonstrates that industry can work together to voluntarily fund, build, and manage a global supply chain security network.

2. The *largest commercial real-time supply chain security project* ever undertaken. During Phase One, sixty-five participants across three continents monitored 818 containers through eighteen tradelanes.

3. A *global network* based on best-of-breed active RFID and other technologies that can become a platform for integration and innovation.

4. *Focused on real-world operational and economic results*—test cases were developed and data gathered using real containers containing real goods bound for destinations in the U.S., Europe, and Asia. Leading authorities on the execution of the supply chain and security analyzed this data.

Assumptions

SST Phase One participants approached the challenges of securing the global intermodal freight transportation system with some fundamental assumptions:

- Industry could not be burdened with excessive regulation or cost such that it breaks the back of global trade. Conversely, industry could not afford to delay action in searching for security solutions.

- Real-time visibility into the status and location of shipments increases efficiency in the supply chain, which leads to substantial economic benefits for all participants.

- Information on the execution of the supply chain must be transparent—the physical chain of custody must be tightly linked with a virtual chain of information, and that information must be available to authorized participants on a strict need-to-know basis.

- It is not possible, in terms of time or financial investment, to completely eliminate risk.

Phase One Network Implementation

Implementation of the Smart and Secure Tradelanes initiative is taking place in progressive phases. SST Phase One was initiated in July 2002 and completed in June 2003. SST Phase Two is in its initial phases and is intended to conclude mid-2004.

Among the first objectives of SST Phase One was to design an information network that would:

- Tightly couple the chain of custody to a chain of information in real time through automated data collection

- Be compatible with legacy systems that were implemented for business or political reasons

- Enable "plug-and-play" of existing and emerging process and technology solutions

To build the network, SST adapted active RFID and other technologies already in use by the U.S. Department of Defense (DoD). This solution, called the Total Asset Visibility (TAV) network, has been in active use since 1991 to monitor military shipments around the globe. In addition to the DoD, SST members reviewed best practices developed by freight consolidators, UPS and FedEx.

Leveraging existing technologies and best practices accelerated and simplified network implementations. Concept to implementation of eighteen tradelanes took only three and a half months.

The primary components of the SST Phase One network were:

- *Wireless networks.* The SST wireless networks were based on active RF (Radio Frequency) and GSM (cellular / Global Systems for Mobile communication). The RF networks used the 433.92 MHz frequency, which was selected because of its known performance metrics (based on its use in the DoD TAV network), broad acceptance, and high performance in challenging supply chain environments, where speed, effective propagation around metal, and ruggedness are essential.

The SST network consisted of fixed and mobile RFID readers that covered sixty-four critical nodes across eighteen tradelanes. These critical nodes function as one or more of the following:

- Point of origin/containerization

- Port of loading

- Transshipment port, if applicable

- Port of discharge

- Point of destination or deconsolidation

Like TAV (see "Case Study: Operation Enduring Freedom/Operation Iraqi Freedom"), the SST network is extensible and can be device-agnostic, enabling continuous innovation that allows industry to choose a mix of best-available technologies and processes.

- *Smart Containers.* Eight hundred and eighteen intermodal containers were affixed with electronic seals that included intrusion/tamper detection sensors (to detect the status of high security bolt seals) and active RFID tags (for two-way system authentication, and communication of location and container status). Each sealing event generated a unique and random sealing event ID that was captured in both the electronic seal on the container and the TSS software (see *Software*, below), making it theoretically impossible to spoof the seal.

  Electronic seals automatically reported their identification and security status to stationary or handheld RFID readers at each critical node, which led to a virtual chain of information that was tightly coupled with the physical chain of custody.

- *Software.* The Web-based Transportation Security System (TSS) software was used to record container routing and scheduling plans prior to loading. The containers were then monitored in TSS at each of the four (or five) critical nodes using data received by the SST network and EDI feeds. All events were logged in an audit log. Unexpected deviations immediately triggered alerts to notify authorized parties.

  Layered security controls were implemented in TSS, including personnel authorization and authentication at the critical point of stuffing, and "virtual border" risk analysis checks at ports of loading. The TSS federated database architecture enabled chain of information sharing on a strict need-to-know basis, and secure (encrypted) connectivity between supply chain participants, who typically would not be readily accessible to each other. TSS was designed for connectivity and collaboration between:

  - Manufacturing and distribution operations

  - Shippers and service providers

  - International terminal operators and domestic terminal operators

  - Shippers and terminal operators

  - All of these participants to domestic and international government entities

  - Potential interagency and government-to-government connectivity

- *Other network components.* Additional components included: network connectivity using Internet and wireless standards such as 802.11B; computer hardware, such as Unix servers from Sun Microsystems and integrated wireless terminals; and industry-standard network and application software, such as J2EE-based application servers from BEA, and SQL relational databases from Oracle.

Phase One Operational Test Findings

SST Phase One operational tests were launched in November 2002. Within only three and a half months, SST implemented a network that can be a platform for innovation and integration across eighteen tradelanes. By the time operational tests were completed in June 2003, SST demonstrated improvements in both supply chain security and efficiency.

"As-Is" Process Findings

The following anecdotes were gathered during interviews conducted at the beginning of SST Phase One. They reflect typical operational problems and vulnerabilities associated with "as-is" supply chain processes:

- One importer stated that it receives only sixty-five percent of the required supply chain data. Of the sixty-five percent, approximately thirty percent was inaccurate, untimely, or incomplete. This significantly impacted the effectiveness of the data for critical operational decision making.

- When using legacy systems to track containers, one large multinational shipper factors in a transit time deviation of six and a half days for a specific tradelane. Only three days are factored in for material deviations, such as a late ship. The other three and a half days compensate for process and information latencies.

- Another participant often receives arrival notices days after a container arrives at a specific inland rail terminal.

- Security experts, government officials, and supply chain operators cited the human element as the greatest vulnerability.

SST Phase One operational testing exposed further problems with existing processes:

- Instructions to check mechanical seals for tampering were correctly followed in only fifteen percent of test cases.

- Five percent of tested containers deviated significantly from their assigned routing.

- Container dwell time at points of origin ranged from 1.5 hours to over 12 hours.

- Shipment manifest data is typically paper based and manually collected well after a container leaves the point of origin.

SST Network Findings

Implementing SST procedures and active RFID technologies had positive effects on supply chain security and efficiency. Analysis of the positive security and operational effects of implementing SST included:

- Timeliness: Information generated by the SST network was more timely than existing processes. In one example, EDI data lagged automated SST data by two days.

- Accuracy: Of the containers tracked end-to-end, 100% were found to have correct and accurate container, route, and manifest data associations within the TSS software.

- Completeness: A substantial portion of manifest entry was enabled at the point of origin through the Web-based TSS application.

- Completeness: The automatic creation of detailed audit logs ensured accountability and created a basis for forensics analysis.

- Location tracking: The SST network was able to identify the location of containers in real time. In one example, a shipper was able to locate and reroute recalled products while in-transit.

- Alerts: Within three seconds, the TSS network checked for security risks and verified handling instructions. The TSS software was able to deliver a go/no-go signal and alerted relevant participants when there were any discrepancies.

- Process: The SST virtual border process eliminated the need for expensive, time-consuming, and unreliable manual checks of high security bolts.

- Process: All new point of origin security and business processes (user authentication and access controls, sealing, shipment information, and so on) were completed with minimal incremental delay to existing business processes.

- Process: Manifest information was aggregated across all supply chain and logistics partners far upstream.

- Process Manifest information was stored centrally in the TSS software, where it was shared on a strict need-to-know basis with authorized parties.

- Process: TSS was shown to be able to automatically transmit 309 manifest information to U.S. CBP's AMS for 100% compliance with 24-Hour AMR.

The initial deployment of SST functionality enabled continuous improvement. Improvements made during the tests were:

- Usability: Training materials for the TSS software were improved early in Phase One, and the software is in the process of being localized for different regions. The menus on handheld readers were simplified with screen icons to make them language independent.

- Reliability: False-positive tamper alerts were resolved by optimizing the intrusion/tamper detection sensors, and by prototyping new form factors for the electronic seals that prevent accidental damage.

- Network availability: GSM (Global Systems for Mobile Communication) was not widely available in the U.S. This was solved by deploying wireless LANS. GSM availability was not an issue in Europe or Asia, where GSM wireless infrastructures are prevalent.

- Durability: Industrial, ruggedized handheld devices replaced commercially available PDAs, which were vulnerable to damage in ports and yards. Electronic seals were prototyped with a new form factor to eliminate the risk of accidental damage.

- Data integration: Synchronizing container tracking data from EDI and other sources and modes was addressed by the TSS software, which enabled event and data management and reconciliation through its business logic and real-time event management functions.

Economic Analysis

Since importers and exporters drive typical supply chain service provider relationships, the focus of the analysis was on the costs and benefits to this important constituency. Based on Phase One economic modeling, the general conclusion is that active RFID is a deployable and affordable technology that is suitable for a global supply chain security and efficiency network.

Dr. Hau Lee and his colleagues at the Stanford University Global Supply Chain Management Forum applied proven inventory models and analytic techniques to the data. Methodologies and analyses included: "what if" scenario and sensitivity analysis: best, likely, and worst cases; Stanford University theory of safety stock and inventory; Stanford University theory of inventory visibility; and inventory-customer service tradeoff analysis. When provided the option, analysts used conservative data inputs and variables.

SST Phase One Estimated Potential Benefits

A single end-to-end SST move of a typical container nets $378-462 of potential value to the shipper when subtracting the operating and variable costs. This amounts to 0.54-0.66% as a percentage of average total container value shipped in SST phase I[1]. The per container potential benefit ranges to a typical shipper in SST Phase One are summarized as follows:

Area of Potential Benefit	Potential Benefit as a Percentage of Avg Total Container Value	Potential Per Container Benefit
Reduction in Safety Stock	.25 - .30%	$173 - 211
Reduction in Pipeline Inventory	.13 - .16%	$91 - 111
Reduction of Service Charges	.08 - .10%	$56 - 68
Administrative Labor	.04 - .05%	$31 - 38
Reduction of Pilferage, Inspections, Loss	.04 - .05%	$28 - 34
Total	**.54 - .66%**	**$378 - 462**

[1] Based on average container cargo value of $70,000.

This model assumes that the average cargo value of containers routed through the top ten importing tradelanes is $70,000. Operational benefits will be higher for shipments valued over $70,000; low-value commodities might not derive meaningful economic benefit.

The financial model developed for SST concludes that there are significant potential economic benefits derived by the SST security solution for a typical shipper. While the ability for shippers to capture these potential benefits will vary, the model substantiates the hypothesis that security and logistics efficiency are closely associated.

This model also demonstrates that shippers can comply with emerging security requirements while reducing logistics costs and/or increasing profits by optimizing the inventory-customer service tradeoff.

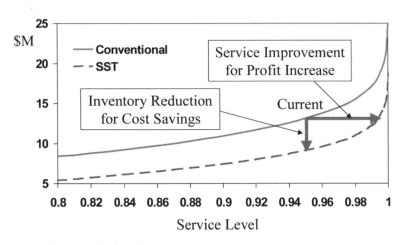

FIGURE 1   Improving Service and Inventory

The real-time security automation functionality of SST could give shippers the flexibility to decrease inventory safety stocks, increase customer service levels, or both. Shippers in turn could then optimize this tradeoff based on their relative position in the market.

Shippers that are market leaders may be more inclined to leverage SST value by decreasing safety stocks since the opportunity cost of losing an additional customer in such markets is relatively lower. Conversely, a firm in a more competitive environment may attempt to increase market share by providing better customer service and fewer stock-outs.

About SST Participants

SST Phase One deliberately sought to work with participants from a large number of vertical industries and countries. Sixty-five organizations participated in SST, including nineteen shippers from nine vertical markets.

Total Participants	65	
Shippers	19	
Ports	13	
Service providers	12	
Carriers	11	
Technology vendors	10	
Breadth of SST Initiative		
Tradelanes	18	
Continents	3	
Industry segments	9	

Port operators included Hutchison Port Holdings, PSA, and P&O Ports, which together account for more than seventy percent of intermodal trade.

Seaport operators	Ports
• Hutchison Port Holdings	• Hong Kong
• PSA	• Singapore
• P & O Ports	• Rotterdam
• China Merchants Holdings International	• Felixstowe
• Stevedoring Services of America (SSA)	• Antwerp
	• Seattle-Tacoma
	• Long Beach
	• Los Angeles
	• New Jersey
	• Charleston
	• Savannah
	• Houston

In addition, SST members participate in numerous U.S. government, international, and cross-border programs and pilots. These organizations and programs include:

- U.S. Bureau of Customs and Border Protection (CBP): Container Security Initiative (CSI)

- CBP: Customs-Trade Partnership Against Terrorism (C-TPAT)

- CBP: 24-Hour Advance Manifest Rule (24-Hour AMR)

- U.S. Transportation Security Administration (TSA): Operation Safe Commerce (OSC)

- Joint Container Working Group (CWG) of the U.S. Department of Transportation and U.S. Customs and Border Protection

- International Standards Organization (ISO): ISO/TC8

- International Maritime Organization (IMO): International Ship and Port Facility Security Code (ISPS)

- Asia-Pacific Economic Cooperation (APEC): Secure Trade in the APEC Region (STAR)

- Container Handling Cooperative Program (CHCP)

- APEC: Bangkok-Laem Chabang Efficient and Secure Trade (BEST)

- World Customs Organization (WCO): various international pilot programs

- European Union: Safe InterModal Transport Across the Globe (SIMTAG)

Appendix B

The Sun EPCglobal Network Architecture

Courtesy: Sun Microsystems

Chapter 1: Introduction

The Electronic Product Code (EPC) and the EPC Network are intended to help businesses improve asset visibility and help ensure product safety and integrity across the supply chain. Companies not only need to know where their assets are, but also need to share that information with their trading partners to deliver seamless, efficient, and secure business transactions. The EPC Network enables trading partners to track and trace items automatically throughout the supply chain. This provides businesses with an unprecedented real-time view of their assets and inventories anywhere, thereby enabling significant gains to operational efficiencies and brand protection efforts. The EPC Network supplies benefits beyond operational efficiencies by enabling safe and secure supply chains with applications that address counterfeiting, tampering, terrorism, and regulatory compliance, among others.

This document describes the architecture for enabling the EPC Network. The architecture is specifically designed to address large-scale implementations in enterprises that need to integrate real-time data flowing in from existing business processes and back-end enterprise systems using Automatic Identification (Auto-ID) tag technologies such as Radio Frequency Identification (RFID) tags. This architecture is part of the Sun EPC initiative, which encompasses software, hardware, services, and best-of-breed partnerships to help create comprehensive solutions for the enterprise.

The Sun EPC Network architecture is built with Sun Java Enterprise System software, which delivers a set of shared technology components and component products for enhanced integration and simplified maintenance. The Java Enterprise System provides an integrated set of industry leading network services that virtually all businesses need today, at a single, annual license fee for software, support, maintenance, consulting, and education services.

Chapter 2: EPC Network Architecture

The architecture for enabling the EPC Network is shown in Figure 1.

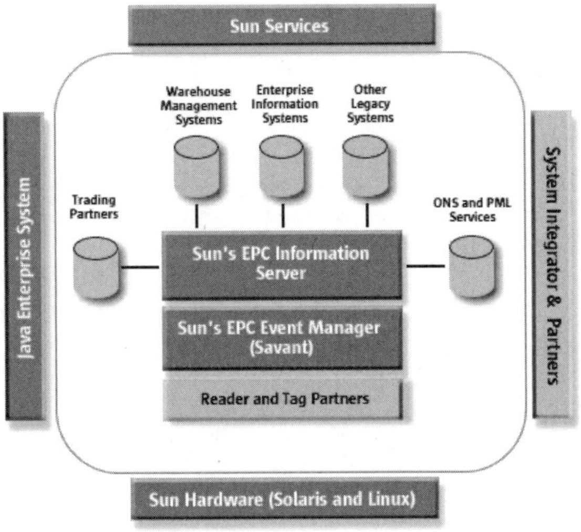

FIGURE 1   Sun EPC Network Architecture

At the bottom of the stack are tag readers or sensors that are responsible for reading tagged items, which may be on a shelf or may be moving through a portal such as a door or cross dock. Each reader continuously reads many tagged items and sends that data to the EPC Event Manager (Savant) for processing. For each reader, typical throughput is approximately 200 reads per second.

The next layer in the architecture stack is Sun's Savant middleware, the Sun EPC Event Manager, which is designed to process streams of tag or sensor data (event data) coming from one or more reader devices. Sun's implementation of the Savant middleware has the capability to filter and aggregate data prior to sending it to a requesting application. For example, a tagged object that is sitting in front of a reader without moving generates many redundant reads. The Sun EPC Event Manager's filters can be programmed to throw out any data that shows the tagged object in the same place, and trigger an action or event only when there is a change in state for the object. For example, an action is triggered when the object moves or a new object comes into the reader's view. The Sun EPC Event Manager can be programmed with other types of filters to enforce specific business rules, as well. Once the filtering has occurred, relevant data may be persisted for use by other layers in the Java Enterprise System stack.

To localize reader traffic, an enterprise may have numerous instances of the Sun EPC Event Manager at each geographically remote site, such as a store, distribution center, or warehouse. A typical store or warehouse is likely to have many readers. Given the amount of network traffic from readers, it is important to localize data by enabling the Sun EPC Event Manager servers to filter the tag data at each site, instead of sending it over the Internet. In addition, it is good practice to isolate the readers from the Internet for security reasons.

The third layer in the Sun architecture stack is the Sun EPC Information Server. Sun advocates that integration technologies be used to connect the Sun EPC Event Manager layer to enterprise information systems (EIS) such as legacy, enterprise resource planning (ERP), warehouse management systems (WMS), supply chain management (SCM), and customer relationship management (CRM) systems, as well as other applications that might want to use tag information. These include components and technologies that comprise the Java Enterprise System, such as Web, application, communication, and security services, and Java technologies such as the Java Message Service (JMS) and the Java 2 Platform, Enterprise Edition (J2EE™) Connector Architecture (CA) to enterprise information systems. Data translation as well as business process management may be needed to enable EIS systems to optimally leverage the real-time information collected and forwarded by the Sun EPC Event Manager. Depending on the specific requirements, either session beans or servlets can be written to run on the Sun Java System Application Server platform.

The topmost layer in the architecture stack is comprised of EIS systems such as ERP, WMS, legacy systems, and proprietary enterprise systems. These must accept and integrate data and events received about tagged objects. As part of the standard EPC Network architecture, it is planned that there will be EPC Information Servers (IS) that hold and disseminate product information in the Physical Markup Language (PML) format. The rest of the paper discusses each of the stack's layers in more detail.

The Sun EPC Event Manager—The Savant

The Sun EPC Event Manager is a key component of the EPC software stack. It is based on version 1.0 of the Savant standards, which were developed as part of the Auto-ID Center Software Action Group (SAG). The Sun EPC Event Manager adheres to the basic 1.0 specifications, and provides additional features and functionality that are specifically designed to address large-scale, enterprise implementations.

Let us first look at the functionality that the standard Savant was envisioned to provide, and then at how the Sun implementation (the Sun EPC Event Manager) adds value.

Sun's EPC Event Manager is a key component of Sun's EPC software stack. It is based on version 1.0 of the Savant standards that were developed as part of the Auto-ID Center's Software Action Group (SAG). The Sun Savant, i.e. Sun's Event Manager for EPCs, adheres to the basic 1.0 specifications and provides additional features and functionality that are designed specifically to address large scale enterprise implementations.

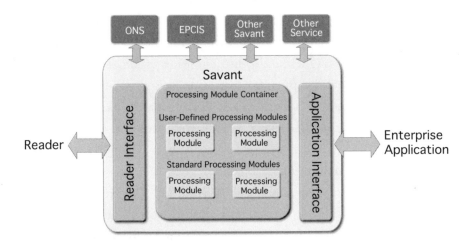

FIGURE 2   Basic EPC Savant Architecture

The Savant is primarily responsible for processing data from RFID tags with a unique EPC that describes a tagged object's manufacturer, product type, and serial number. The Savant provides the following benefits:

- It provides an interface that enables RFID readers and other network devices or sensors to be connected to the EPC Network.

- It helps integrate RFID event data with the EIS by defining a set of interfaces that facilitate sending and receiving real-time data to and from these systems.

- It provides a general-purpose, event routing system.

Essentially, the Savant is a data collector and a router that performs operations such as data capture, data monitoring, and data transmission. For each reading, the Savant gathers a minimum amount of information such as the tag's EPC, the EPC of the reader that scanned the tag, and the timestamp. Specific requirements for EPC processing vary from application to application, so the Savant is defined in terms of processing modules or services, each of which provides a specific set of features and may be combined to address specific application requirements. Since the emphasis in the version 1.0 specification of the Savant framework is on extensibility rather than specific processing, it defines only the most basic processing modules, and lays out a framework within which user-defined processing modules can function. This modular architecture facilitates innovation without committing—at this stage—to a monolithic specification that attempts to satisfy universal requirements.

The Sun EPC Event Manager was designed to allow for flexible deployment capabilities without sacrificing availability, scalability (both horizontal and vertical) or manageability. One characteristic that makes the Sun EPC Event Manager unique is its distributed architecture.

A fundamental tenet of distributed systems is that they must be able to accommodate changes that may occur on a network. Compute resources on a network, such as a server or other networked device, may fail or die. Sometimes a new compute resource may be introduced to the network. As a result of the preceding actions, applications executing on a particular compute resource may perform poorly or fail completely. This is very similar to the situation experienced in large scale enterprise Auto-ID and EPC network deployments. For example, a warehouse reader may go down unexpectedly, or a server may be knocked over by a forklift. Since distributed systems are designed to inherently accommodate the vagaries of compute resources connected by a network, the Sun EPC Event Manager is also designed around this type of architecture.

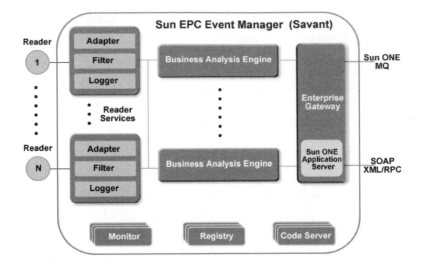

FIGURE 3   Sun EPC Event Manager Architecture

The Sun EPC Event Manager implements what is known as a federated service architecture, which essentially provides distributed, self-organizing, and network-centric capabilities. These building blocks enable a dynamic, distributed architecture capable of adapting to unforeseen changes on the network. This architecture also makes the Sun EPC Event Manager highly scalable. For example, individual services or components—the Reader Service or Registry—may be distributed to run across multiple computing resources on a network.

Additionally, this architecture is resilient. If a reader or other computing resource is physically disabled or damaged on the shop floor, the Event Manager continues to work by dynamically provisioning and relocating software services from the disabled computing resource to another compute resource on the network.

Some key components of the Sun EPC Event Manager are:

- *Device Adapter*: This layer enables devices from many different manufacturers, such as RFID or bar code readers, to communicate and interact with the Event Manager.

- *Filters*: These assist in deciphering useful data from the noise constantly generated by tagged objects. Filters may also contain small pieces of process or business logic. Standard filters are provided for event smoothing, event batching, event changes (tags in and out), and event pass/blocking.

- *Loggers*: These are somewhat similar to device adapters, except that loggers are used to notify external systems of RFID and non-RFID event data. The Sun EPC Event Manager provides standard loggers that log information either to the file system, a JMS queue, or through XML, http, and SOAP messages.

- *Enterprise Gateway*: This component is used as the common interface for enterprise applications requesting data from the Sun EPC Event Manager.

Sun EPC Information Server

The Sun EPC Information Server provides access to significant business events generated by the Sun EPC Event Manager. It also serves as an integration layer that offers several options for integrating the Sun EPC Event Manager with existing EIS or custom enterprise applications. Direct connections from the Sun EPC Event Manager layer to enterprise applications can result in the creation of information silos within a company. Using the Sun EPC Information Server between the Sun EPC Event Manager and back-end applications allows for maximum flexibility when business requirements or enterprise applications change. Using software and APIs that are part of the Java Enterprise System enables developers to quickly and flexibly integrate EPC data with enterprise applications.

Data from the Sun EPC Event Manager feeds into the Sun EPC Information Server, where it is stored and made available in a consistent manner to any application that needs it. This approach increases overall system reliability and flexibility, while reducing maintenance and support costs. It also provides a suitable location for correlating EPC events to business logic. Another benefit is that the Sun EPC Information Server can be used to implement additional functionality, such as data reformatting and data warehousing.

The Java System Application Server provides three options for point-to-point integration with EIS systems, meaning it ties a Savant server to an EIS system. These options are:

- J2EE CA

- Asynchronous reliable messaging through the Java Message Service

- Native support for Web services

The J2EE CA, which is part of the J2EE platform (version 1.3 onwards), defines a standard way to tightly couple an EIS system with either a Web application or Web service. With the appropriate connector installed, an application can employ the functionality of the EIS without having to deal with the complexity of integrating remote access, transactions, and security. The functionality of the EIS appears as just another service provided by the application server.

In the case of the J2EE CA, the EIS or custom system is tightly coupled to the application. This means it can make a call to the EIS, much like it would make a call to a database, via JDBC technology. To the Web application or Web service using the J2EE CA, the EIS looks like a local resource, a familiar paradigm that eases the developer's task. Additionally, the Java System Application Server can take care of underlying system issues such as pooling, security, and transaction support.

The disadvantage of tightly coupled integration is that many times it is not appropriate, because unlike a database, the EIS may take a relatively long period of time to make updates. For example, integration with a supplier's ordering system may require human intervention before receiving a response to an order request, which could mean holding the connection open for days. In cases where connections are held open for a long period of time, a loosely coupled approach where asynchronous messages are sent and queued to the EIS is more appropriate.

For loosely coupled integration, the Java System Message Queue, which is included in the Java System Application Server, provides the standard JMS asynchronous reliable messaging mechanism for integrating Web applications or Web services with an enterprise's Message-Oriented Middleware (MOM) environment. This facility allows Java Enterprise System applications to exchange messages with the EIS.

The third option is provided by the platform's native support for Web services. By their nature, Web services easily cross machine and software boundaries, and so are well-suited for solving integration problems. Because the EIS and Web service running on the Java System Application Server view each other as Web services, they can interact using standards such as the Simple Object Access Protocol (SOAP), Web Services Description Language (WSDL), and Universal Description, Discovery, and Integration (UDDI).

These approaches provide flexible options to integrate the EIS to Savant servers with point-to point integration for a narrow or single purpose. The developer could write workflow logic into an Enterprise JavaBeans (EJB) stateful session bean or servlet to tie multiple EIS systems together using the integration options previously mentioned. This is an excellent approach to consider if the business process is straightforward and fairly static.

Tightly Coupled Integration   As previously mentioned, the J2EE CA defines a standard architecture for connecting the J2EE platform to heterogeneous EIS and custom applications. It addresses the key issues and requirements of EIS integration by defining a set of scalable, secure, and transactional mechanisms that enable the integration of EIS with service containers and enterprise applications.

With the J2EE CA, a service container and connector (and underlying EIS) can collaborate to keep all system-level mechanisms—remote access, transactions, security, and connection pooling—transparent to the application. The J2EE CA provides the most direct mechanism for integrating the Sun EPC Information Server with an EIS. This mechanism results in a close coupling between the two, providing both high performance and high reliability.

Loosely Coupled Integration   The Java System Message Queue provides asynchronous reliable messaging through the coordination of the following main components:

- Administered Objects
- Client Runtime
- Messaging Service

ADMINISTERED OBJECTS   Administered Objects encapsulate provider-specific implementation and configuration information in objects that are used by client applications. Such objects are created and configured by an administrator, stored in a name service, accessed by client applications through standard Java Naming and Directory Interface (JNDI) lookup code, then used in a provider-independent manner.

The Java System Message Queue provides two types of administered objects: ConnectionFactory and Destination. While both encapsulate provider-specific information, they have very different uses within a client application. ConnectionFactory objects are used to create connections to the Java Message Service, while Destination objects identify physical destinations. Administered Objects make it easy to control and manage a Message Service because the behavior of connections can be controlled by requiring client applications to access preconfigured ConnectionFactory objects through a JNDI API lookup.

The proliferation of physical destinations can be controlled by requiring client applications to access only those Destination objects that correspond to existing physical destinations. This arrangement provides control over Java Message Service configuration details. At the same time, it allows client applications to be provider independent. They do not need to know about provider specific syntax, object naming, or configuration properties.

CLIENT RUNTIME   As the second main component of the messaging system, Client Runtime provides client applications with an interface to the Java Message Service by supplying them with the JMS programming objects. It supports all operations necessary to enable clients to send messages to destinations and receive messages from them.

THE JAVA MESSAGE SERVICE   The Java Message Service provides the core functionality of the asynchronous reliable messaging system. It is made up of the following main components:

- *Broker*. A broker provides delivery services for the messaging system. Message delivery relies upon a number of supporting components that handle connection services, message routing and delivery, persistence, security, and logging. The Java Message Service can employ a single or multibroker configuration.

- *Physical Destination*. Delivery of a message is a two-phase process—delivery from producing client to a physical destination maintained by a broker, followed by delivery from the destination to one or more consuming clients. Physical destinations represent locations in a broker's physical memory and persistent storage.

PML and EPC Information Service

This section briefly describes the still-evolving Physical Markup Language (PML) and the EPC Information Service standards.

PML development is part of the Auto-ID Center effort to develop standardized interfaces and protocols for communication with and within the Auto-ID infrastructure. The Auto-ID PML Specification 1.0 defines syntax and semantics.

PML provides a standardized, XML-based format for the exchange of EPC data and consists of two parts:

1. *PML Core*: Describes raw data received from tags and sensors

2. *PML Extensions*: May be used to associate arbitrary information with physical objects

In the end, PML provides a common, broadly hierarchical method for describing physical objects. For instance, a particular vendor's beverage might be described as a Carbonated Beverage, which falls under the subcategory Soft Drink, under the broader category of Food. Not all classifications are so simple, so to ensure that PML has broad acceptance, the Auto-ID Center relies on work already completed by other standards bodies. PML does not attempt to replace existing vocabularies for business transactions or other XML application libraries, but does complement these with definitions about EPC Network system-related data.

Types of PML Data   In addition to product information that does not change (such as material composition), PML includes data that changes constantly (dynamic data) and data that changes over time (temporal data). Dynamic data in a PML file might include the temperature of a shipment of fruit. Temporal data, such as an object's location, changes throughout an object's life. Making all of this information available in the PML enables companies to employ information in new and innovative ways. A company could, for instance, set triggers so the price of a product falls as its expiration date approaches. Third-party logistics providers could offer service-level contracts indicating that goods are stored at a certain temperature.

EPC Information Service   The EPC Information Service essentially makes EPC Network-related data available in PML format to requesting parties with appropriate authorization. Data available through the EPC Information Service may include:

1. Data collected from the Sun EPC Event Manager through readers or sensors

2. Specific data about the tagged object such as date of manufacture, weight, expiration date, and so on

3. Product catalog information

In responding to requests, the EPC Information Service obtains information from a variety of data sources that already exist within an enterprise before translating that data into PML format. So an EPC Information Service may be a simple Web service front-end to an EIS.

Java Enterprise System

Bringing the best in Java Web and application services together, the Java Enterprise System delivers enormous value to IT organizations by helping to reduce both cost and complexity. It provides all the core enterprise network services needed to build a secure, scalable, and highly available Java technology-based application or service. Enterprise network services are the capabilities that sit between the traditional operating system—such as the Solaris OS or Linux OS—and business applications. Enterprise network services are engineered and deployed to meet business requirements for a scalable, interoperable, available, and secure IT software infrastructure. This enables IT organizations to focus on business logic development when deploying business solutions.

The Java Enterprise System delivers a set of shared technology components and component products for enhanced integration and simplified maintenance. The Java Enterprise System is offered at $100 per employee, per year. This single low price eliminates the complexity of managing multiple pricing structures for multiple software products, support contracts, and service agreements, making it easier for customers to acquire, deploy, and run the software they need. This single annual license fee covers software system, support, maintenance, consulting, and education services.

The Java Enterprise System and services help customers spend more time focusing on their business requirements rather than integrating and supporting a myriad of point products. Customers gain better control and increased business agility while benefiting from reduced IT costs and complexity through the Java Enterprise System's simplicity, predictability, and affordability.

The core set of the enterprise network services that the Java Enterprise System delivers are:

- *Web and Application*: Based on J2EE technology, these services maximize application reuse and developer collaboration, enabling IT organizations to develop, deploy, and manage applications for a broad range of servers, clients, and devices.

- *Network Identity Services*: Used to improve security and protect key corporate information assets, these services help ensure that appropriate access control policies are enforced across all communities, applications, and services on a global basis.

- *Portal*: Provide anytime, anywhere access capabilities to user communities, delivering personalization, aggregation, security, integration, mobile access, and search. Portal services enable mobile employees, telecommuters, knowledge workers, business partners, suppliers, and customers to securely access their personalized corporate portal from anywhere outside the corporate network through the Internet or extranet.

- *Communications and Collaboration*: Specific capabilities include messaging, real-time collaboration, calendaring, and scheduling in the context of the user's business environment.

- *Availability*: Enables the predictability and resilience that businesses expect from their application infrastructure. Availability services also provide the patented "Always-On" technology for application and Web services, delivering extremely high-quality service and massive scalability.

- *Security Services*: Delivers the peace of mind business today demands. Security services provide consistent single sign-on to online resources. They protect content using the latest security standards and resilient authentication and access control options.

Components   The following components comprise the 2004Q2 release of the Java Enterprise System. Additional components will be added in future releases.

- Java System Directory Server 5.2

- Java System Identity Server 6.2

- Java System Directory Proxy Server 5.2

- Java System Application Server Platform Edition 7

- Java System Application Server Standard Edition 7

- Java System Message Queue Platform Edition 3.5

- Java System Message Queue Enterprise Edition 3.5

- Java System Web Server 6.1

- Java System Portal Server 6.3

- Java System Portal Server Mobile Access 6.3

- Java System Portal Server Secure Remote Access 6.3

- Java System Messaging Server 6.1

- Java System Calendar Server 6.1

- Java System Instant Messaging 6.2

- Cluster 3.1

- Sun Cluster Agents for System components: Web, Application, Directory, Messaging, Calendar Servers, and Message Queue

Software Service and Support   Sun's consulting, proactive support, and in-depth education services help customers architect, implement, and manage their Java Enterprise System environment. Sun Services offers comprehensive architecture, implementation, and management services and methodologies that enable customers to take full advantage of the Java Enterprise System. Sun Services provides customers with technical support, software maintenance, installation services, custom consulting, and comprehensive education to ensure a smooth transition and integration of the Java Enterprise System into their enterprise.

Summary

The Sun EPC Network architecture is specifically designed to address large-scale, enterprise Auto-ID EPC deployments. The architecture can scale from a single small site with a few readers to many geographically dispersed sites with multiple readers at each site. The Sun EPC Event Manager is uniquely designed for enterprises with reliability, scalability, and manageability in mind, providing an integration layer that further allows scaling of EPC Network infrastructures. It provides many options for incorporating tag data and events with existing business processes and EIS systems. The Java Enterprise System is a radical new approach that changes forever the way businesses acquire, develop, and manage software. Using the Sun EPC Network architecture in the Java Enterprise System infrastructure can deliver many business benefits. Only Sun has the experience and the end-to-end portfolio to deliver such a unique and industry-revolutionizing strategy. With the Java System, EPC information is integrated into essential business applications faster, easier, and at a lower cost than ever before—so you can focus on innovation, competition, and bottom-line results.

Chapter 3: Best Practices

Sun encourages the following best practices and steps when pursuing an Auto-ID EPC deployment:

1. Empower a multidisciplinary team: A dedicated team with executive sponsorship is important to the success of any Auto-ID EPC deployment or pilot. Many companies underestimate the effort required to undertake an Auto-ID EPC project. Because the project can often be complex, it requires the cooperation of executives and senior-level managers from IT, Engineering, and Operations departments.

2. Define a simple and measurable business issue: What are the business goals that the enterprise wants to achieve with its deployment? Given the emerging nature of Auto-ID EPC, it is best to find a contained compelling application for Auto-ID within the four walls of the company that offers the most value to the organization. Addressing labor-intensive tasks such as asset tracking, shrinkage-reduction, and inventory threshold (out of stock) applications are popular pilot projects.

3. Scope out data and business processes: An accurate understanding of existing data and business processes at the outset of any Auto-ID EPC project is crucial to success. Without knowing how a business process works today, companies will find it difficult to implement and track changes.

4. Select partners: Trying to manage everything by yourself can be daunting, so it is essential to leverage your partners' experience. Why build expertise in areas that are not likely to be part of your core competency, when you could be focusing on those aspects of the project that are more critical to your company's bottom line?

5. Map network architecture and enterprise integration: Most companies start with readers and tags as part of their Auto-ID EPC pilot. However, this causes them to get bogged down with physics experiments. Therefore, it is important to think early on about the overall network architecture. Assuming that the tag reads are figured out, think about how data will flow from the reader and integrate with the EIS systems. This may actually help you better understand overall system requirements and even what type of readers and tags infrastructure is required.

6. Determine the right readers and tags: Once the data requirements and overall network architecture are mapped, specify the readers and tags requirement. Key factors include material (metal or liquid), size of items to be tagged (cases or pallets), application (global asset tracking, local shrinkage problem), environment (indoor or outdoor, temperature and moisture), regulatory (what frequency is legal in which part of the world), and human or psychological factors (how does this affect stakeholders).

7. Prototype: Start small and see how all the pieces come together in a test environment. Compare data from existing processes. Test your assumptions and make sure you are seeing the hoped-for improvement.

8. Implement: Once you have necessary data from the prototyping efforts, go ahead and implement the new system.

Chapter 4: Conclusion

The EPC Network holds the promise to significantly improve supply chain productivity by providing unprecedented visibility—a real-time view of assets and inventories wherever they are located. This visibility can enable companies to track and trace goods from the original manufacturer through distribution points and on to the retailer. This information can be integrated into business critical applications, or shared with supply partners, and can provide dramatic gains to operational efficiencies and brand protection efforts.

While creating a cost-effective way to generate and collect product data is a significant challenge, so is integrating it into the EIS and ERP systems and repositories. Modern businesses rely on multiple back-end applications to run their business, and many of these will need access to the data feeds from Savants distributed across company operations. Rather than creating new, standalone modules, Sun's architecture for EPC Networks integrates EPC data with existing applications—those used to run your business today.

As an early sponsor and leader of the EPC Network technology, and Sun has participated in some of the first trials with leading consumer goods manufacturers and retailers. With over three years of experience, Sun technology and expertise—along with best-of-breed partners—are helping companies with a range of solutions. Whether you need a proof of concept or a production deployment, Sun can help your company, too.

REFERENCES AND RECOMMENDED READING

AIM, Inc. Shrouds of Time: The History of RFID. By Dr. Jeremy Landt. Available at *www.aimglobal.org*

Brown, Patricia, and Beth Bacheldor. *Roundtable: Tagging RFID Gains*. Optimize, February 2004, 67-70. Available at *www.optimizemag.com/issue/028/issues.htm*

Case Study: Wal-Mart's Race for RFID. eWeek, September 15, 2003.

Combating Counterfeit Drugs, A Report of the Food and Drug Administration. U.S. Department of Health and Human Services. Food and Drug Administration. February, 2004. Available at *www.fda.gov/oc/initiatives/counterfeit/report02_04.html*

Department of Defense Guide to Uniquely Identifying Tangible Items. Office of the Principal Deputy Under Secretary of Defense. Available at *www.acq.osd.mil/log/logistics_materiel_readiness/organizations/sci/rfid/rfid_reference.htm*

DLA RFID Pilot Update. Presented to DoD/Industry Association Meeting, April 2004. Available at *www.acq.osd.mil/log/logistics_materiel_readiness/organizations/sci/rfid/assets/Meetings/Industry%20Association%20Brief%20pilots.pdf*

Finkenzeller, Klaus. *RFID Handbook*. Second Edition. Chichester, England: John Wiley & Sons, Ltd., 2004.

Frequently Asked Questions, EPCglobal. Available at *www.epcglobalinc.org*, *www.epcglobalus.com*

Future Store Initiative. Metro Group. Available at *www.future-store.org*

Goods That Talk, Strategic Impact of RFID (Online Seminar: "Meting the Retail RFID Mandate"). A.T. Kearney, February 26, 2004. Available at *www.atkearney.com*

Identification Friend-or-Foe (IFF). Available at *www.nrl.navy.mil/content. php?P=FRIENDFOE*

International Organization for Standardization. *www.iso.org*

Juels, Ari, Ronald I. Rivest, and Michael Szydlo. *The Blocker Tag: Selective Blocking of RFID Tags for Consumer Privacy.* Available at *www.rsasecurity.com/*

Proc, Jerry. *ASDIC, RADAR and IFF Systems Aboard HMCS HAIDA.* Available at *http://webhome.idirect.com/~jproc/sari/sarintro.html*

Radio Frequency Identification (RFID) (formerly ANSI NCITS 256-2001). National Resource for Global Standards. Available at *www.nssn.org*

Radio Frequency Identification (RFID) Policy and - UPDATE, Supply Chain Integration, Office of the Assistant Deputy Under Secretary of Defense, October 2, 2003, February 20, 2004, July 30, 2004. Available at *www.acq.osd.mil/log/logistics_materiel_readiness/organizations/sci/rfid/rfid_policy.html*

Sarma, Sanjay E., Stephen A. Weis, and Daniel W. Engels. *RFID Systems and Security and Privacy Implications.* Available at *www.autoidlabs.org*

Safe Harbor. U.S. Department of Commerce. Available at *www.export.gov/safeharbor*

SMART DUST, Autonomous sensing and communication in a cubic millimeter. Available at *http://robotics.eecs.berkeley.edu/~pister/SmartDust*

Target Issues RFID Mandate. RFID Journal, June 2003 and Feb 2004. Available at *www.rfidjournal.com*

United States Department of Defense Suppliers' Passive RFID Information Guide. Available at *www.acq.osd.mil/log/logistics_materiel_readiness/ organizations/sci/rfid/supplierguide.html*

Venture Development Corporation. *A White Paper On Radio Frequency Identification (RFID) Middleware Solutions: Global Market Opportunity*. Prepared by Michael J. Liard

Wal-Mart updates RFID road map, revises expectations for '05 deadline. Computer World, May 19, 2004. Available at *www.computerworld.com/printthis/2004/0,4814,93266,00.html*

Wal-Mart's RFID Edict Ripples Through IT. Info World, November 21, 2003.

INDEX

THIS BOOK IS SAFARI ENABLED

INCLUDES FREE 45-DAY ACCESS TO THE ONLINE EDITION

The Safari® Enabled icon on the cover of your favorite technology book means the book is available through Safari Bookshelf. When you buy this book, you get free access to the online edition for 45 days.

Safari Bookshelf is an electronic reference library that lets you easily search thousands of technical books, find code samples, download chapters, and access technical information whenever and wherever you need it.

TO GAIN 45-DAY SAFARI ENABLED ACCESS TO THIS BOOK:

- Go to **http://www.phptr.com/safarienabled**
- Complete the brief registration form
- Enter the coupon code found in the front of this book on the "Copyright" page

If you have difficulty registering on Safari Bookshelf or accessing the online edition, please e-mail customer-service@safaribooksonline.com.

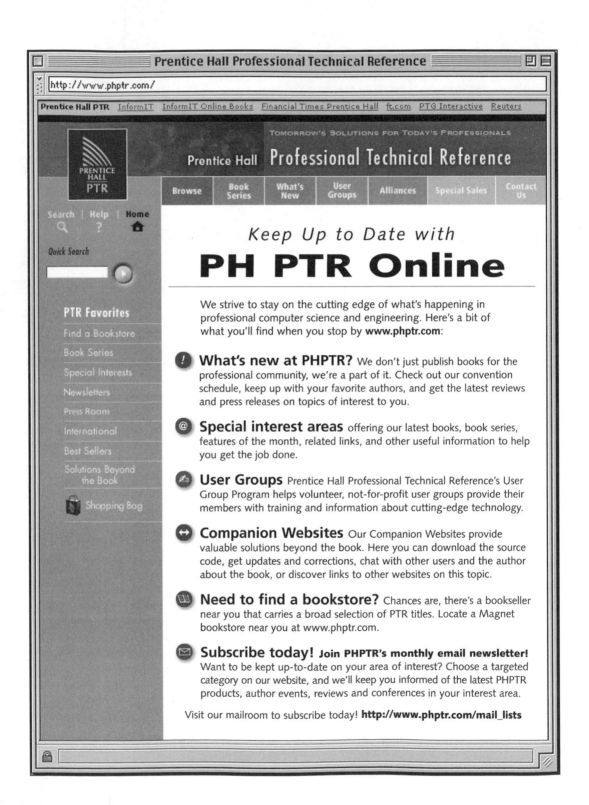